The Smart Investor's Money Machine

The Smart Investor's Money Machine

Methods and Strategies to Create Regular Income

BILL KRAFT

WILEY

John Wiley & Sons, Inc.

Published by John Wiley & Sons, Inc., Hoboken, New Jersey.
Published simultaneously in Canada.

For general information on our other products and services or for technical support, please contact our Customer Care Department within the United States at (800) 762-2974, outside the United States at (317) 572-3993 or fax (317) 572-4002.

Wiley also publishes its books in a variety of electronic formats. Some content that appears in print may not be available in electronic books. For more information about Wiley products, visit our web site at www.wiley.com.

Library of Congress Cataloging-in-Publication Data:

Kraft, Bill, 1943-
   The smart investor's money machine : methods and strategies to create regular income / Bill Kraft.
       p. cm. – (Wiley trading series)
   Includes index.
   ISBN 978-0-470-39174-7 (cloth)
   1. Investments.   2. Stocks.   3. Securities.   I. Title.
   HG4521.K686 2009
   332.6–dc22

                                                                                    2008045551

Printed in the United States of America.

10 9 8 7 6 5 4 3 2 1

*This book is dedicated to Patti, to Billy, to Laurie, to Jeanne,
to Joe, to both Christas, and, of course, to Sunshine.*

Contents

Preface

I have been trading and investing for a living since the 1990s. Those activities have helped me to enjoy a wonderful lifestyle, but it was not always that way. For many years, I spent 10- or 12-hour days, 6 days a week engaged in the practice of law. I must admit that during much of that time I had a very good income, but it came at a price. Part of the price was time away from children and family. I look back on those times as my children grew up and realized that I had missed so much. There was the time my daughter saved the game in Little League with a great catch, and I wasn't there to see it, and the times I missed my son's junior high football games while I worked to try to help solve someone else's problems. I know many readers are likely to share similar regrets, but those times are past and can never be recaptured. Meanwhile, the money came and the money was spent with little thought to the future and to retirement.

As age advanced and I quit the practice of law, I began a search for a more satisfying life. I always loved photography so I bought a photo processing and portrait studio franchise only to see the photo world turn digital and watch most of my savings that were invested in the store and equipment diminish with every passing day. As it turned out, the business had little to do with photography and everything to do with retail. If I thought I had been a slave to the practice of law, it was nothing compared to the demands of a retail business, which required even more hours per week than the practice of law and for a significantly smaller financial reward. In fact, the biggest paycheck I remember taking from the photo business was $200 even after our store was named "The Best of the Best" for three consecutive years. I did come away from the photo business with great and newfound respect for the small business owner, but decided it was not for me. I finally was able to sell the store for a fraction of my investment and began a search for a new career.

Ultimately, I was drawn to trading stocks and options and that became my passion. It has helped me move from near financial ruin to what some consider an enviable lifestyle. Now, I am blessed to have homes in the Colorado mountains, overlooking Hanalei Bay on Kauai, and in the Sonoran

Desert. My commute is from my bedroom to my office, which, depending on the house, is a distance of from 10 to 30 feet. On the average, I spend a couple of hours a day trading and have plenty of time to devote to family, hobbies, and volunteer work. I do some private coaching on a limited basis and occasionally I am asked to speak by various trading organizations. All in all, my time is much more my own than it ever was in the past.

WHAT TO EXPECT

This is my second book, so the inevitable question is whether it is a rehash or update of my first book, *Trade Your Way to Wealth*. While I do address certain strategies like closed end funds, writing covered calls, and selling naked puts and spreads that I discussed in the first book, I have tried to look at them in greater depth and definitely from a different perspective. In this book, I will examine those strategies more from the perspective of an investor rather than that of an active trader, but I'll include specifics on ways to adjust trades like naked puts and naked calls for the investor who may want to be more active. *Trade Your Way to Wealth* was designed as a primer for traders with an emphasis on risk and risk aversion, while this book emphasizes the creation of additional streams of income and how they can be managed depending upon the reader's own lifestyle.

This book deals with a number of additional methods to create income streams that are unrelated to option trading. Some investments we'll explore here may have an added benefit of offering the ability to trade options in addition to the income available from the basic method, but the investor will be able to create an income stream whether he chooses to use options or not.

As we proceed, you will see examples of hypothetical investors of different ages with different needs, lifestyles, and perspectives. While I have painted them with a broad brush, the reader may place himself along the spectrum depending on his own station in life in order to apply approaches that fit his current status and abilities. In general, we can expect that the investor who is married with young children will look at things differently from a new college graduate or from a retiree with grandchildren. My goal here is to introduce investors to an investment strategy or strategies that can work for them in their own unique circumstances. In the world of investments, there is something for almost everyone, and one of the keys is to find what fits you in whatever your current circumstances may be.

My objective is to show the reader how they can build their own "money machine." It will not be the same machine for everyone, but almost anyone will be able to build such a machine. The parts of the machine will often be different depending on who you may be and where you are in life, but the end product can be the same—added cash flow. Your money machine may not result in instant riches, but it can help improve your financial state almost from the beginning. We are looking at the "eat the elephant" approach to wealth accumulation. It can rarely be done in one bite, but it can definitely be done one bite at a time.

I hope that you can use this book in a variety of ways. First, it may help you target types of income-producing investments that fit within your personal time constraints. In Chapter 5, for example, we'll look at some high-yielding investments for people who have little time to devote to their investments. Chapter 6 adds strategies for the investor who has a little more time and the desire to be more proactive. Next, you may also discover investing vehicles that you had not considered before. Some examples like Master Limited Partnerships (Chapter 5) that offer the potential of significant tax-deferred income or tax-free municipal bonds (Chapters 5 and 8) or zero coupon bonds (Chapter 8) as a method of financing a future college education, or annuities and even reverse mortgages (Chapter 9) that can provide lifelong streams of income are just some of the subjects that may work for you. Finally, once you have explored the possibilities, you will find specific ways you can utilize these methods and strategies in constructing your own money machine.

In essence, this book will show you a variety of methods you can use to produce regular added income. The methods vary widely and encompass a wide range of choices. Some choices will require a fair amount of effort and one, at least, will require attention only once in the investor's life. As in almost all investing, there are trade-offs between things like risk and reward, time spent and potential returns, and knowledge and method. Only the individual can decide which strategy or combination of strategies are right for him.

As an aside, you may already have noted that I am referring to investors using masculine pronouns. I am only doing that to avoid the awkwardness of statements like "he or she may choose to buy ... " or "when he or she researches ... ," and so on. When I speak before large groups, I would estimate that 90 percent of the audiences are men so I have chosen the masculine rather than the feminine simply because such a high percentage of investors seem to be male. I definitely mean no offense to women and readily admit that many women are excellent traders and investors.

There is one important caution for the reader to observe and that is to be aware and to understand that the statistics, prices, yields, and trades mentioned throughout the book will not be the same by the time you read the information. Prices and yields vary from moment to moment so whenever I write about a specific trade, it is just a snapshot in history to be viewed only as an example. The reader should also remember that just as prices change, so, too, do companies. Please do not take the mention of any particular company as any kind of a recommendation. By the time you read this book, circumstances will have changed. Companies may be better or worse or may no longer exist. New opportunities constantly arise and it is those we must seek.

WHAT THIS BOOK WON'T DO FOR YOU

This book is not a blueprint to get rich quick. Application of the methods set out here may, however, help you get rich steady. Unfortunately, there seems to be a perception among many who are new to trading or who have been trading unsuccessfully that there is some secret that will lead to instant riches. The truth is that instant riches are unlikely and patience is a prime ingredient to building wealth. I recall that after my first book came out someone commented on Amazon.com that the title was false advertising because although it was a very good book on the basics of trading, no one would get wealthy using low- and no-risk strategies. I beg to differ and I am living proof. The whole title of that book is *Trade Your Way to Wealth: Earn Big Profits with No-Risk, Low-Risk, and Measured-Risk Strategies*. The self-anointed critic failed to account for measured-risk strategies that might lead to riches faster, but that also were accompanied by higher risk. The low-risk and no-risk strategies also can be used to garner big profits and to lead to wealth, but it is a steady progression, not an instance where the elephant is eaten in one huge chomp.

Those who seek the holy grail of investing are likely to encounter little but disappointment. If there is a holy grail of trading, it is not some secret mathematical formula or hardly known strategy kept as a closeted secret to be revealed only to a chosen few. Rather, it is the acquisition of investing knowledge and the regular, steady application of that knowledge. Countless strategies, systems, and methods are sold to the investing public with an implied promise of infallibility. Someone always is selling another foolproof proprietary algorithm that is sure to bring riches. If we really think about it, what trading system could have predicted 9/11, or the timing and failure of Lehman Brothers, or the subprime crisis? What is tomorrow's news? If I had tomorrow's news, I wouldn't go to the stock market first, I'd buy a lottery ticket. Clearly, no system can predict the news and news is something that definitely can move the markets. If a system can't predict something that moves the market, how can it predict the market reaction?

I believe that the presumption that there is a holy grail of trading is responsible for a great deal of anguish among traders seeking it. There seems to be expectancy on their part that if they keep searching they will ultimately be rewarded with some secret and incredibly profitable system. When their searches continually turn up nothing and losses mount or portfolios vanish there is nothing but pain and frustration. To be clear, if you are looking for a secret holy grail of trading or investing in this book, you simply won't find it. It doesn't exist.

I am often asked exactly what I do as I trade. Though I am willing to share my methods and strategies, I rarely do because what I do will always be different from what you do. Trying to copy someone else's trades, something I call clone trading, just doesn't work very well. If you wanted to try to copy my trading, ask yourself why when you consider that my goals are different from yours, I am likely a different age, my risk tolerance is different from yours, our level of knowledge will not be the same, our capital will be different, the time we can or are willing to devote to our investments will be different, and so on. The goal is to create your personal money machine; not Bill's.

WHAT YOU *WILL* BE ABLE TO DO

As you read this book, you will be exposed to a broad spectrum of income-producing investments. I suggest you think of them as parts of the money machine you want to build. In great part they are interchangeable, but some will require more time and effort on your part in actually running the machine. Others may require very little time, but the trade-off might be a smaller income flow.

In my estimation, successful investing always starts with introspection. Take a good look at who you are, what you really want, what you are willing to do to get it, realistically, what time do you have to devote, and how interested are you in the overall concept and any of the specific money machine parts?

Once you have performed the self-evaluation, you can use this book to see what parts are available that fit your qualifications. Undoubtedly, for one reason or another, you will reject certain strategies. You may not want to undertake the risk attendant to trading naked options, or you may not have the time needed to monitor spread positions, but you may really like the relative ease and tax advantages of owning municipal bonds or the high yield of some Real Estate Investment Trusts (REITs). The parts are here; it is up to you to decide what will work best in your circumstances.

Beyond identifying the parts you want, you will also be able to see ways to use them to your own advantage. If spreads interest you, for example, you will learn not only what they are and how to enter them, you'll learn important considerations about how to trade or adjust the positions as they develop. If bonds interest you, you'll learn strategies for trading them to achieve specific goals such as creating cash that is available when it is time to pay for college or to create a regular, predictable cash flow.

If you become interested in active trading, in Chapter 10 you'll see my personal outlook on what I believe are important trading concepts and some keys to trading success. I'll also cover a number of things I believe are overrated. In the Suggested Reading at the end of the book, you'll see a number of books that I have found helpful to my own investing education and without which I probably would not be where I am today.

I am confident that you will find methods in here that will enable you to add income flow to your life. I know that more income can help nearly everyone. I hope that what you find in the chapters that follow convince you to go forward to help yourself better your own economic circumstances.

BILL KRAFT

Acknowledgments

When it comes time to write the acknowledgments I know my work on my book has neared its end. Thinking back from the time the project began until the end, I realize how much support I have had. As was the case with my first book, I owe Kevin Commins of John Wiley & Sons a debt of gratitude for setting the hook and getting me started on this project. Thanks, too, to Emilie Herman, my fantastic editor for her great ideas and gentle guidance throughout the writing process. Thanks, as well, to the many other folks at Wiley, some whose names I know and many I don't for their efforts in getting this book to print.

I've dedicated this book to my family and I want to acknowledge them here as well. Thank you, Patti, for being my love. You make each day a wonderful adventure. Billy and Laurie, I am very proud of you; congratulations on the way you are living your lives, it brightens my days. Thank you for your support. Joe and Jeanne, thank you for making my kids happy and for being such wonderful spouses. It all helps me along my way as well.

Little Christa, you are a wonder and even when I was struggling over some problem or other as I wrote this book, you made me smile as you always do. Thank you.

Thank you, too, to my friends who have been so supportive of me. You make my life easier and that makes writing easier.

Finally, thank you, Sunshine, for your love and loyalty. Without you lying at my feet as I wrote, I'm sure this book would never have been finished.

B.K.

The Smart Investor's Money Machine

Build a Money Machine

This book first emphasizes the need and the reasons for investors to look out for themselves, add to their income, and take control of their own finances. Part I addresses how we can get extra income by creating a money machine to generate regular additional income for the investor. This machine can be designed and created specifically by the individual after considering his own needs and abilities. The first three chapters are intended to show the reader how he can move forward to improve his life by committing to the betterment of his own financial welfare through the creation of these money streams. The first part, then, addresses the concept and decision-making elements.

In Part II, the reader will examine a wide array of specific investments that he may choose to use alone or in concert as parts for the money machine he designs for himself. In that second part, we'll see precisely how different methods and strategies may be incorporated and utilized to reach an objective of adding income to almost anyone's life.

CHAPTER 1

How We Get the Income We Need

I 've been rich and I've been poor. I've had good paying jobs and I've been broke twice in my life. I've never been homeless, but I've been to the point where I couldn't pay the mortgage—let alone the phone bill, the electric bill, the car payment, or the credit cards. Along the way, I've learned many financial lessons. Among them are:

- You aren't likely to get rich working for someone else.
- No matter how good you may be at your job, you are expendable.
- If you are an employee, your time is not your own.
- Politicians may promise, but government won't take care of you.
- The term "security" can be an illusion.
- No one cares as much about your money as you do.
- It's probably better to learn to manage your own money than to rely solely upon brokers, financial planners, or insurance salespeople.
- Social Security isn't secure.
- You would be wise first to learn how and then create multiple sources of income.

During most of the years when I practiced law, I enjoyed a very good income. At the same time, however, there was an important trade-off. My time was not my own. As Abraham Lincoln said: "A lawyer's time and advice are his stock in trade." My time did not belong to me if I wanted to earn money. My time belonged to my clients and was controlled by them and by the courts. Vacation dates, for example, were ruled by court calendars, and nights with family were sometimes abandoned because of municipal meetings or zoning hearings. I'm not seeking sympathy because I knew I was trading time for cash, but I often wondered whether there might be some better way to achieve those qualities of life that financial health can bring without sacrificing my time to control by others.

It seems clear to me that anyone who has a boss, anyone who is an employee, is faced with the same situation. They are relinquishing control of their own time to their employer. Certainly the employer is entitled to that control because he is paying the employee for the employee's time and effort. In fact, the employer has every right to tell the employee that he no longer needs the time and services and can fire the employee. I have been on the short end of that stick as well as having been the person doing the firing. While neither side is pleasant, it can be devastating for the person who has lost his job. For most, the sale of their time, their job, is the only source of income and once lost the income stops. That is how I became poor one time.

NEARLY EVERYONE NEEDS INCOME

Most of us need income. Baby boomers coming to their later years need food, shelter, medical care, insurance, and transportation just like anyone else. Certain costs like those for medical care are rising dramatically with no end in sight and the older we get the more we are likely to need additional care. Transportation costs have risen and the costs of fuel may continue to rise for as long as we continue our dependence on carbon fuels. Food costs are also rising as crops like corn and sugar that once were relatively cheap become more costly as they are converted to alternative fuels. There is only so much land on which crops can be grown and when more of that limited acreage is grown in corn and less in wheat, it is no surprise that the cost of flour will rise. The use of corn for food now competes with the use of corn for fuel so while supply may remain nearly constant, demand has increased significantly. In addition, the demand for energy has risen around the globe. Factors like these guarantee higher costs of living with the passage of time.

Over the past several years, I have spoken to many in the 60-plus age group who are approaching retirement or who have retired. A high percentage of those people are concerned that they may outlive their money or that they may have to diminish their quality of life to live within their means. Previously undiagnosed conditions like Alzheimer's disease raise the possibility of long-term care and the large expenses associated with the treatment. These fears are real as people live longer and inflation erodes fixed income streams. Some already find it necessary to take part-time jobs just to get health insurance benefits. Baby boomers who once looked forward to a pleasant retirement now need to focus on how they will be able to afford the rest of their lives. Later in this chapter I'll discuss some of the possible solutions and their potential effectiveness.

Certainly baby boomers are not the only group who can foresee a need for continuing and, perhaps, additional income. Young families are also burdened by heavy expenses. While their costs for medical care may not reach the same levels as that of their elders, costs for food, shelter, transportation, and insurance will probably exceed those of the preceding generation. In addition, they must face the explosion of costs in education and, in a high percentage of homes, the costs of day care. Today, in families where both spouses are in the household, it is common for each to have at least one job and a significant proportion of one of the incomes frequently goes to day-care costs if there are children. In homes split by divorce it is probably even more common to see both parents employed. In all of these situations, the families must face the issues and costs of day care and make decisions whether the cost might outweigh the benefits of income from one spouse's job. Where there is a stay-at-home mom, the family must weigh income needs against their view of the desirability of child care from a parent versus child care from an outsider. In addition to those issues while children are young, parents also consider the costs of education for their children.

Private school tuitions can be extremely burdensome. The current kindergarten tuition at the east coast school where I attended high school is now $17,600 and the tuition for high school is almost $24,000. At current rates at that school, the total tuition to send one child from kindergarten through high school would be well above a quarter of a million dollars. Not far from where I now live in the Colorado mountains, one school I checked charges tuition of $3,500 for kindergarten and $5,150 a year for first through eighth grades. Private college tuitions are also very high. As I write, the University of Pennsylvania, an Ivy League school ranked fifth by *U.S. News & World Report* for 2008, charges tuition and fees of almost $36,000 a year plus a little over $10,000 for room and board. By contrast, Briarwood College in Iowa (ranked 38th among Baccalaureate Colleges in the Midwest for 2008 by *U.S. News & World Report*) charges about $20,000 for tuition and an additional $5,900 for room and board. State universities and colleges, though significantly less expensive particularly for in-state students, nevertheless can be fairly costly. Mississippi State University, for example, ranked in the third tier of national universities in 2008 by *U.S. News & World Report*, charges in-state residents almost $5,000 in fees and tuition plus almost $7,000 for room and board.

Single people who are not committed to any relationship do not escape the need for income. They, too, must have shelter, food, transportation, and the necessities of life. Frequently, they have additional expenses to enhance their enjoyment of life. Dating, meals out, entertainment, and furnishing apartments or homes, education loan payments, and credit card bills (shared by almost every category) all add to the need for income.

Income needs can be daunting. According to the U.S. Census Bureau, the median annual household income in 2006 was only $48,201. It is really no wonder that so many have a hard time getting ahead, let alone making ends meet.

ONE SOURCE OF INCOME IS NOT ENOUGH

Undoubtedly the most common source of income is a job. Most of us have gone to school and learned that we need to get a job and have been taught that is how we need to make our livelihood. How much we can earn at our job or jobs is dependent on many factors. Generally, education can play an important part, as can the number of hours we devote to the employment. Geography is also a factor and, according to U.S. Census figures, the median household income in New Jersey in 2006 (the highest ranking) was just short of $67,000 while in Mississippi (the lowest ranking) it was slightly over half that at $34,343. While employment is clearly the predominant source of income for most people, it does come with a number of limitations. As I discussed earlier, during the hours of employment, the employer owns your time and exercises very significant control over your activities. At least as early as 2007, I saw that some employers track their employees' movements by GPS. This demeaning practice may assure greater productivity, but to my mind it makes being an employee less desirable.

Even professionals who have control over the operation of their businesses are beholden to their clients or patients. As we know all too well, there are only so many hours in the day and we can't work all of them so no matter what our hourly rate, our earnings from employment do have a cap. While we can earn large sums from employment, we also run the risk that we may lose clients, lose our job, or suffer an injury or disability that prevents us from continuing to earn at the same level. At the same time, a job can also offer at least the illusion of security. When we have a job, we have an expectation that we will regularly get a paycheck and we may even have the promise of a pension at retirement.

Although times are changing, when we think of the employed, we tend to think of the traditional work force; those in the 18 to 65 age bracket. However, because of the need for income, many older people are continuing to work longer or are finding new careers or new jobs. Social Security simply isn't enough. The term is approaching oxymoron status. I was recently reading *The Reagan Diaries* (HarperCollins, 2007) and was reawakened to President Reagan's efforts to get Congress to do something about the Social Security program as far back as the early 1980s. In a March 26, 2008, article entitled "Officials warn of Medicare's demise," Richard Wolfe, in *USA Today*, wrote simply:

> *Medicare and Social Security are going broke.*
>
> *That was the blunt message delivered again . . . by trustees for the two programs. Each year they warn of the impending doom caused by benefits that will eventually exceed revenue. . . .*
>
> *Social Security, the insurance program for nearly 50 million retirees, survivors, disabled workers and their dependents, will start spending money it's not raising in 2017 and go bust in 2041 unless Congress acts.*

This once important source of income for the elderly has long been nothing but a political football and is fast becoming a joke. When a suggestion was made that people become responsible for managing part of their own retirement there was a great hue and cry from the politicians and even, to my great surprise, from the AARP. People just can't manage their own money was the argument (as if government could). Politicians have offered no alternative proposal to repair the system and lash out at anyone who dares suggest that people might take care of their own money. The year 2017 is just over the horizon and nothing is being done to save Social Security. Instead, the benefits are reduced or postponed or taxed again. Seemingly we forget that these funds were originally taken as a tax from paychecks to be returned, with interest, to those who paid. The bottom line is that the baby boomers and those who follow should not and cannot count on the past promises of Social Security and will receive only a pittance, if anything, to assist their income needs if things stay the same. In the meantime, contributions from current workers must not only help provide for their own future, but also must assist in financing the retirement of the older generation.

Another potential source of income for retirees is the pension—where it has been properly funded, the company still exists, and the employee has managed to remain in his position long enough to be vested. Many in my own generation were taught that if you went to work for a corporation and faithfully fulfilled your duties you would be set for life. In some cases that expectation has been fulfilled. Sadly, in others, the expectation has been dashed. Friends of mine have suffered varying fates because they followed a long-term plan designed to result in a comfortable retirement with a decent pension. One such friend was a longtime faithful employee of WorldCom. His reward, instead of the pension he deserved and earned, was a company that went down the tubes with a chairman who was convicted of fraud, conspiracy, and filing false documents with regulators all relating to an $11 billion accounting scandal. Another friend who served his company long and well was simply fired shortly before his pension vested. That fine man not only lost the pension rights he had worked for, he was so injured psychologically that he became a complete recluse. Again, pensions can and do provide a source of income to those who have earned them when the company treats its employees honestly, stays in business, and properly funds and manages the pension. I have friends who have been and continue to be the happy beneficiaries of such situations. Again, as with Social Security, it is great if you get it, but like so many things in life, it may be unwise to count solely on income from such sources. The Bureau of Labor Statistics published data demonstrating that individuals born between 1957 and 1964 held an average of 10.8 jobs from age 18 to 42 (BLS News Release, "Number of Jobs Held, Labor Market Activity, and Earnings Growth Among the Youngest Baby Boomers: Results from a Longitudinal Survey." Washington, D.C., June 27, 2008). As I see it, that number is likely to increase because of earners taking on more part-time work and second jobs and changing jobs and careers more often. Not only do fewer jobs offer pensions, but also the frequency with which workers change jobs means pensions are less likely to be vested even where they do exist. These factors make it even more important that people create additional streams of income for themselves.

We need to be aware that there are many ways to produce streams of income besides a job. Devices as common as savings accounts and certificates of deposit (CDs) also offer income through the interest they pay, but generally speaking, while relatively safe, the rates are something short of spectacular. Corporate bonds sometimes offer decent rates of return and municipal bonds are available where the interest is free of federal and sometimes state taxes. In later chapters, I'll discuss some of those vehicles as well as ways to utilize the stock and options markets to generate income.

When I was an active lawyer, I enjoyed one stream of income: my job. After I left the profession and opened a photo-processing and photo franchise, my income came from that source alone and I quickly learned that although I loved photography the business had little to do with that passion and all to do with the retail trade. As anyone in the retail business knows, endless hours must be devoted to succeed. Though my store was rated "The Best of the Best" by the franchisor, the time and energy did not translate into great profits. While working more than 60 hours every week, I think the largest check I ever took out of the business was about $200. My employees made at least minimum wage while I, as the owner, didn't. Even with significant revenue, little filtered down to the bottom line after sales taxes, property taxes, wages, Social Security payments, rent, equipment leases, inventory, and the franchisor's percentage were paid.

During that time, I was too close to the situation or not smart enough to realize there had to be a better way. As we worked harder and harder only to get deeper in the hole, one of life's cataclysmic events occurred and made me realize that I could achieve more if I worked smarter, not harder. Since I did not want to start over in the practice of law in my fifties, I sought other work. I tried sales and did quite well, but again, my time belonged to others. Finally, I stumbled upon stock and option trading, studied it, and achieved financial success. Now, at least, I could rule my own time. As I studied, I learned that the truly wealthy made their money work for them and frequently had several streams of income. My eyes were opened wide by Robert Kiyosaki and Sharon Lechter's *Rich Dad, Poor Dad* (New York: Warner Books, 2000) through which I learned the valuable lesson that my time was not the only asset I could use to produce income. My thinking changed and my approach to earning broadened. Through the wisdom of others, I came to the realization that I could attain higher levels of income and better assure financial security by using assets in addition to my time to produce additional income.

Since that time, I have gone from someone whose income was totally dependent upon his time to a person with several streams of income. I use my time to set up trades and investments and then let them provide income through interest, dividends, and premiums I generate with certain option strategies. I also invest some time in coaching traders and investors as they work to improve their own trading. I have three subscription services where I publish some of my stock and option trades to try to show others some of the methods and strategies that have worked for me. I also have been able to invest in some resort real estate and am able to enjoy rental income as I look forward to appreciation. I have created and sold DVDs of trading seminars I conducted, and I receive royalties from my books. Some of these income streams still require my time, but nowhere near the hours I used to spend practicing law or running a small business. My trading activities require no more than 10 hours or so a week and that includes sending alerts about some of my trades to subscribers. The resort property is managed by an agent and requires almost no time. Once a book is written, I may have some speaking engagements to assist in the promotion, but I find that those few instances are fun for me and not very time-consuming. I take on no more than 10 coaching students a year so that endeavor involves about 20 days and a little follow-up with e-mail and phone conversations.

In short, I am now blessed to be in a position where I am financially comfortable, secure, and able to utilize my time as I choose. I now have time for family. I can play golf or go fishing almost whenever I want and it is a rare day, indeed, when I can't do pretty much as I please. I try to remain mindful of my own good fortune and make an effort to give back through some charitable activities. Much of this has come because I have learned how to create a number of income streams and, in this book, I am going to try to show you ways in which you may be able to do the same things.

ADD STREAMS OF INCOME WITHOUT ADDING ANOTHER JOB

I am now in my mid-sixties and am interested in working less and enjoying more while at the same time trying to assure a strong flow of income. It doesn't matter what stage you may be in life, you probably have similar goals. Whether you are a baby boomer or a newlywed getting ready to raise a family, you very likely need income. Wouldn't it be great if you could create income by using sources other than, or at least in addition to, your time? You could then have more time for your family, your avocations, your charities, or whatever else may draw you. Almost certainly, your stress level would be reduced since the financial pressures you may feel now would not be as great. In short, the quality of your life could be improved.

I believe each of us should take the personal responsibility to learn how to create income by using assets in addition to the sale of our time to an employer. Once learned, we can go on to create income sources that will help us in our quest for a better quality of life and financial security.

In this book, I am going to try to show you ways to create additional income. Some of these ways may not be new to you, but may give you a new perspective. Other strategies may be eye-openers; things you have not yet considered or, maybe, have not yet taken the time to understand fully. As you read through this book, you will probably find some methods or strategies that are more appealing to you than others; some you may reject out-of-hand for now, but want to explore later. Whatever the case, hopefully, you will have at least peeked at some possibilities of adding to your income.

The emphasis throughout the book will be on investment vehicles related to the stock, bond, and option markets. Though worthy of mention and something I do myself, I will not focus on real estate investing except in relatively general terms. There are already a large number of books dealing with real estate investments and I would defer to them for specific detailed information on various strategies.

In Chapter 2, I'll discuss how you may want to approach the creation of income-producing assets and ways to formulate a plan for the management of those vehicles depending on factors like age, experience, time, and interest.

In the chapters that follow, I'll try to focus on specific individual strategies and tactics that can be used within the broader strategy to enhance potential earnings. None of these strategies is new. Most, if not all, have been used effectively and in a variety of ways. I have successfully used every strategy in this book and I continue to do so at the time of this writing. I would urge the reader, as I did in my first book, *Trade Your Way to Wealth* (Hoboken: John Wiley & Sons, 2008) to understand the risks of each strategy and to practice the strategy before putting real money at risk.

 GETTING INTO GEAR

No matter where we are in life, most of us have a need for income. The needs of the young and growing family may differ from those of the baby boomer or the young single person, but they are needs nonetheless. Even though we may have been taught that working a lifetime for a corporation would lead to financial security or that the government would take care of us in our later years, life may teach us otherwise. It is my belief that we have an obligation to ourselves and to our families to learn how to create income sources in addition to what we can achieve by selling our time and particular expertise to our employer. In the end it really is up to us to educate ourselves financially.

This book endeavors to outline a number of ways in which we can create and utilize income-producing assets beyond the sale of our own time.

CHAPTER 2

A Blueprint for Your Money Machine

The truth is, no matter whom you might be, it probably wouldn't hurt to have a little more income. For the vast majority, an additional $500 or $1,000 a month could really make a difference in quality of life. Wouldn't it be great to teach yourself some way or ways to make that car payment or set aside additional money each month for education or retirement or whatever you wanted? You have that ability, if you are willing to add a little knowledge and put aside a little money that you can use to generate added income quite regularly.

There are many ways to have your money work for you rather than have you work for your money. You can build a personal money machine that creates new streams of income if you are willing to do it. That willingness to do it is the first key. It can be done without taking up a lot of time, but it does require that you gain some understanding and then take the actions that are needed.

FIRST, MAKE THE COMMITMENT

The first necessary action is that you make a decision. Make a decision that you are willing to commit some time and some effort to build an income machine that can enhance the quality of your own life and that of your family. Although almost all of us see and appreciate the idea that added income can help make our life more comfortable and give us more free time to do what we want, many of us are unwilling to do what it takes to achieve that goal. I once heard a fine teacher say: "If you are willing to do

13

for six months what others won't, you can do for the rest of your life what others can't." Please think about that for a moment. In Chapter 1, we looked at some of life's expenses; we know that many expenses are high and will probably only get higher. How are you going to deal with those necessary burdens? Doesn't it make sense to make some short-term sacrifices to ease your financial burdens over the long run?

I agree it may not be easy to find the time. Your world may be filled with obligations to your work, your spouse, your kids, your parents, your community, your church, or a myriad of other things, but isn't a primary obligation to yourself and your financial well-being? Could you perhaps set aside a half hour or 15 minutes a day or maybe a couple of hours over the weekend for a few months if the result would change your financial health for the better for the rest of your life? Instead of watching a reality show on TV or reading a romance novel or going to the movies, how about spending that time learning a little about some of the ways you can make more money. Once you have paid your dues by gaining the knowledge, you could reap rewards that are way beyond your current expectations.

Some of us may believe our time could be better spent and choose to spend our time doing other things. Would those folks still shy away if I told them I spent a little time and found a $6,000 investment that could grow into more than $120,000 in 10 years in a Roth IRA? Would they be more interested if I also told them that all they have had to do is to buy a $3 a share REIT (Real Estate Investment Trust) on the day I wrote this and just hold it for the 10 years and they could wind up with that $120,000 even if the stock price stayed the same and the dividends remained the same? That stock is paying dividends at the annual rate of 35 percent based on the price I paid for the shares I own. There is little point in identifying the stock today. The same opportunity in terms of the high dividend will not be available by the time this book gets to you, but quite likely there will be other good possibilities if you can make a little time to do what you need to do.

Others of us may feel that investing is too complex for us and should be left to financial experts. My first answer to that objection is simply that no one cares as much about your money as you do. My second answer is that smart investing is really not particularly complex although some of the financial experts would have you believe it is. According to information gathered by Zacks Investment Services and published by *Smart Money* in November 1996, five out of eight full-service brokers failed to beat the S&P 500 over the three-year study period. You could just buy an ETF (Exchange-Traded Fund) representing the S&P 500 and at least assure yourself of a return essentially equal to the performance of that index and better than 62 percent of the full-service brokers referenced by the Zacks. Just look at how poorly the so-called experts did for themselves at now-defunct companies like Bear Stearns or Lehman Brothers.

You have the potential to add regular significant income streams to your life. Only you can decide whether it is worth the effort. Now is probably as good a time as any to decide.

ESTABLISH THE FOUNDATION FOR YOUR MACHINE

The biggest hurdle a new trader or investor needs to overcome is the vocabulary of trading. After that, in my view, comes the ability to recognize risk and manage it. I spent a great deal of time identifying risk and discussing ways to manage it in my first book, *Trade Your Way to Wealth.* I'll continue to emphasize areas of risk throughout this book and will make every effort to highlight the risks inherent in each income-producing method I discuss.

Ultimately, the battle for success is with oneself. The markets are governed more by the psychological than the logical over the short- to mid-term at least. Investors and traders often make decisions based on emotions, fear, and greed, more than through any predetermined discipline, yet it is discipline that usually wins the day. So one important goal we want to achieve is discipline in our trading. The average retail trader has no edge because his trading responds to the emotions of the trade. Perhaps the cardinal rule of successful investing is: cut your losses and let your profits run. Nearly everyone acknowledges the wisdom of the thought, but only a few actually do it. If a stock we own is enjoying a run, how do we decide when to get out? Some people may feel it has a good profit so they'll just get out only to see the price triple or quadruple from where they sold it. Others may see the price go up to a previous resistance only to turn and drop as they hang on, hoping it will go back up. In the first case, fear played a part in the decision; the fear that profit could be lost if the price turned down resulted in selling a position that had a lot of profit to go. In the second case, greed took the wheel. The trader saw profit and wanted more. Even though the stock signaled a change in direction, the trader was afraid he would miss out on more gain. Meanwhile, he watches his profit turn to loss and now he is afraid to take the loss and it magnifies.

In each case, the trader cut his profits and, in the second example, let his losses run. Unfortunately, that is exactly how far too many traders operate. That phenomenon of cutting profits and letting losses run is the product of emotion rather than discipline. The way to overcome the hurdle is to trade with discipline. Make the decisions before you enter the trade. Decide when you will enter and decide what specific circumstances will cause you to exit. You could decide to enter based on a new high and exit with a trailing stop if the price dropped 6 percent (or 5 percent, or

7 percent, or whatever you picked). Now as the stock moves up, your exit would move up with it. If the stock price turned on you, you would automatically cut your loss. In this latter example, we had developed a plan and that plan removed the dangers of emotion and gave us an edge; a way to cut our loss or let our profit run that was completely detached from our emotions. As with the creation of most machines, our income machine requires that we start with the basics and build from there. The first step in constructing our machine, then, is the creation of a plan. The plan provides the structure within which to act and it supplies the discipline without which we are not likely to succeed.

CREATE YOUR PERSONAL PLAN

In *Trade Your Way to Wealth*, I emphasized the need for a personal plan and tried to show how creating and following the plan could help readers become more successful traders. If you are willing to take the time to create a plan, it will help you attain the discipline necessary to success in the markets. That book was directed more toward the trader than toward the investor and while this book includes a great deal of information about trading, it also includes additional material directed to the investor. I distinguish between trader and investor primarily based on the length of time each perceives they are likely to hold a position and the expectations each may have. I see the investor as one who looks at himself as a buy-and-hold person; someone who expects to buy for the long run while expecting capital appreciation over time and, perhaps, enjoying dividends along the way. I envision the trader as someone who is somewhat more proactive and who expects to be in and out of positions more frequently than the investor. The trader is probably attempting to profit from shorter-term moves, is unwilling to hold through major downward moves in the market, may play both directions, and is seeking to generate income at the same time.

Both classifications (investor and trader) can make handsome profits, but clearly, their plans will differ. Without repeating the detailed examinations of the potential elements of a trader's plan, I set out the following questions in *Trade Your Way to Wealth* that I believe can be helpful in the creation of a personal trading plan:

Will I trade full-time or part-time?

How much risk money will I assign to my trading business?

What are my business hours?

What strategies will I use?

When will I make my trading decisions?

What is the maximum number of trades I will have in place at one time?

What will trigger an entry into a position?

What will trigger an exit from my position?

What types of orders will I use?

What are my expectations?

These elements should also be considered by the investor, but the emphasis and answers to the questions are quite likely to differ fairly dramatically. I once was criticized for failing to include my own personal business plan in *Trade Your Way to Wealth*, but I intentionally didn't include it because it probably has little, if anything, to do with your plan or anyone else's plan. The time I, as an active trader, devote to trading is almost certainly going to differ from the time an investor may spend. I will undoubtedly prefer certain strategies in a bear market and another trader may not even want to participate in a bear market while a true buy-and-hold investor may not care that a bear market is underway. I also will probably be using a different amount of risk money and my time horizons will almost certainly be different. The plan, quite simply, must be personalized to you and to your situation. If you are 35 and I am 65, aren't we going to be looking from much different perspectives? Won't your needs and desires be different from mine? Lastly, the plan is a work in progress. It is something that I return to regularly and adjust. As I gain more knowledge, for example, I may prefer a different strategy in a sideways market than the one I used in the past. As I gain experience, my expectations may change as might the time I am willing to devote to the business.

Long ago, a colleague gave me one of the best pieces of advice I have ever had. He said he thought most people have a weakness in that they have a lot of trouble making a decision. They agonize over the process of making a decision, weighing every "what if" they can conceive. My friend believed it was much better just to make the decision and move forward. Even if that first decision turned out to be wrong, all we need do is make another decision and fix it. That is the way I believe the plan should evolve.

As we examine various strategies throughout the book, you will see how they can be interchangeable parts in your income-producing machine. The plan can be created and revised but the primary purpose of the machine will be to generate income from streams beyond the investor's individual time and effort.

WHAT THE PLAN WILL DO FOR YOU

We have seen that there is a significant benefit to a plan because it does at least two things for us. It permits us to create a structure or framework in which we can perform our investing activity, and it helps to provide the discipline necessary to make a success of it. Those are things a plan does, but what is the purpose that underlies those benefits?

You really are planning so that you can satisfy your needs and reach new goals. Since needs and desires change over time, your plan will be influenced by many factors including time of life, family situation, interest in investing, available time, and desire to add income streams to name just a few. The plan, though, is for you. It is your opportunity to begin to implement your decision to enhance the quality of your life. Added income is in your reach. It really isn't hard to achieve, but it is only within reach if you extend yourself a little by doing a little studying and doing a little planning.

In the remainder of this chapter (and throughout the rest of this book), I am going to discuss examples of some considerations that investors or traders might incorporate in their plans depending on varying hypothetical situations. Factors that may influence each of our decisions might include our age, amount of money we have, our personality, family situation, amount of time we have available, and our level of knowledge. The hypothetical examples that follow are meant only as food for thought to illustrate some variables that might affect the content of an individual's plan to build his money machine. What we are talking about is making more income with less effort than you have expended in the past. Creating a plan that works for you in your life is designed to help you achieve that objective.

BABY BOOMER EXAMPLE: THE BALDINGS

Ed Balding has reached the age of retirement and he believes that his biggest earning years are behind him. He and his wife, Grace, have two grown children and three grandchildren. The kids are doing well and don't need any financial help. Though the Baldings have little debt, Ed has begun to have concerns that he may outlive his money or that he or Grace may need long-term care somewhere down the road and he wonders if their assets will last to pay for that care. Because of those concerns, one important consideration almost certainly must be preservation of capital. At the same time, though, Ed and Grace need to spend money for food, shelter, recreation, vacations, insurance, home maintenance, and property taxes. Ed has a small pension and his 401(k) is pretty nice, but he wishes it were bigger. He does have a couple thousand shares of stock in the company where he worked. Ed and Grace know Social Security is not going to save the day and are concerned they may have to reduce their standard of living a bit as time goes on.

Looking at those circumstances, it seems that the first priority for any plan Ed might create would incorporate some way or ways to preserve capital and, after that, to generate additional income. In terms of strategy, he could consider tools like bonds (Chapter 8), closed-end municipal bond ETFs (Exchange-Traded Funds), REITs (real estate investment trusts), MLPs (Master Limited Partnerships), the latter three in Chapter 5, or maybe optionable dividend-paying stocks so he could insure his positions and maybe sell covered calls (Chapter 4).

In essence, Ed would plan to include only strategies with relatively limited risk but with a significant return. Earlier, I mentioned a REIT that was trading around $3 but was paying an annual dividend around 35 percent. The risk would be the cost of the stock. The return was pretty good. Further fundamental analysis revealed that the book value of the stock was over $5 a share so the breakup value was greater than the stock price giving some modest assurance of safety. Here, in any event, is a limited-risk position that is providing a strong income through the dividend and also offers the potential of capital appreciation. In fact, the stock had been as high as $11 a share before the subprime mortgage fiasco.

As a new retiree Ed might have some extra time so he could plan to add some daily study time or market analysis time and perhaps learn some new strategies to add income. The baby boomer who was interested in trading might look into spreads (Chapter 8) or condors (Chapter 6) as limited-risk ways to enhance income or he might consider selling covered calls (Chapter 4) as a strategy as well as selling them against stock he already owned.

Trading decisions could be made on a daily basis now that there is more time to look at the markets and maybe Ed would decide to take advantage of that additional time and add more trades since he would have the ability to monitor a few more positions.

Will our hypothetical Mr. Balding make his decision to enter a trade based solely on fundamentals or will he incorporate some technical element of timing? Sound fundamentals can certainly be desirable, but they offer no assurance of price movement over the shorter haul. Neither do they tell us when to enter a position. Strong fundamentals may well add some level of security. It is probably safer to own shares in a company that has good earnings, a good dividend history, a reasonable P/E (that is, the ratio of price to earnings), and low debt than a company that has no earnings, a load of debt, and an untested product. The trade-off is that the latter company could strike it rich for itself and for its shareholders, but the risk that it will fail is significantly greater than the strong, staunch, solvent company. As someone who is interested in capital preservation, Ed might want to consider weighting his plan toward the safer bet. Incorporating a decision to look for prospects with sound fundamentals may require a little more time, but, to many, the extra time may be well worth the added benefit. That still leaves us with a question of entry and exit strategy. Fundamentals may help us decide what to buy, but they offer little assistance in deciding when to buy or when to sell.

If Ed doesn't have the time or interest in trading actively, he can still generate income but he would be more likely to choose strategies that require little or no monitoring. He may be content with collecting dividends or perhaps buying bonds (Chapter 8) or an annuity (Chapter 10) to add some income. He is still motivated to preserve capital, but also would like to add income so all he need do is explore avenues that accomplish the goal with less active participation. It usually comes down to deciding what benefits we want and what we are willing to give up in exchange. We could create regular income through laddering bonds or by selling naked puts (Chapter 7), or we can just buy an annuity and let the income flow.

The Baldings may well want to tailor their plan so that it meets the sleep soundly test. In other words, can they generate enough extra income to satisfy their needs without losing sleep over whatever level of risk they have chosen to accept? If they can achieve that end, we are doing well. That is what we are seeking when we create our plan. We are looking for a balance between reward and risk that lets us be comfortable.

While Ed may conclude that he would like to bring in a little more income during retirement and is willing to make some extra effort, after all, this is supposed to be retirement so he doesn't want to make a full-time job of it. His plan might be that he will work part-time, no more than an hour and a half a day, and that he will look things over for an hour after dinner each evening at which time he will make his trading decisions and he will trade for a half hour beginning at 1 P.M. Eastern Time. He will write covered calls against the company stock he already owns and his primary strategy beyond that will be to buy fundamentally sound stocks in bullish sectors while the market is bullish and will sell at-the-money covered calls against those positions. He will enter a new stock position only when the price bounces up off an uptrend line and will exit both the stock and the calls by trailing a stop-loss order 4.5 percent behind the stock price. He will invest no more than 4 percent of his risk money in any particular position. He expects some of his positions will be losers, but overall, looks for a 2 percent per month return on his investment.

There we see Ed's plan. He has incorporated the strategies he will use, the hours he will spend, his entry criteria, his money management plan, and his exit strategy. Each element of the plan is designed to further the goal of adding income while protecting against a significant downside. Could Ed's plan be different? Of course it could. Will yours be different? In all probability it will. Can it be changed? Definitely it can be changed. In fact, it should be reviewed regularly and changed to fit knowledge, experience, and needs.

MIDDLE-CLASS FAMILY EXAMPLE: THE MIDDLETONS

Tim and Mary Middleton have been married for six years, are in their early thirties, have two kids (ages two and four) who are in day care, and both Tim and Mary are employed. Since they are carrying a hefty mortgage, have two car payments, and their credit cards are nearly maxed out, Tim has a second job. How can they plan to get ahead and help educate their children? College is only 14 years away after all.

The different needs and financial circumstances between these folks and our baby boomer example are vast. If we look through the eyes of each of the two families, we can see that it is apparent that they are going to have substantially different plans. Both need income, but the ways they go about it will probably be quite different. One immediate distinction is that the Middletons have no need to preserve capital. They don't have any.

Almost any financial planner would be likely to advise this family to get rid of the credit card debt. If they are paying 20 percent or more in credit card interest, it is going to be hard just to get even let alone ahead so a first priority would be to eliminate the debt. Some people have resorted to home equity loans in the past only to re-amass credit card debt once the home equity loan has been taken. Not a good idea. One good piece of advice that is rarely taken in this world is to tighten the belt and make some sacrifices and that should probably be the first thing undertaken. Next, I suspect attention might be given to the cost of day care compared to the income that cost is generating. As one mother summarized in her blog:

> "... I will be paying $70 per day for 2 kids in daycare. That means I am only taking home $50 per day. Is it really worth it?? I have given some thought to finding a waitress job in the evenings. I figure if I can make $400-$600 per week by working 3 or 4 nights a week we will be much better off than me bringing home $250 with my regular job and I will be raising my kids as well." (http://Colorado-mama. blogspot.com/)

This issue is one that exists in many homes. Does it really make sense to have a job just to pay for day care, or is there enough extra income from the job that it readily takes care of the day care costs?

This book is about creating income and income streams from investments, but it seems that the first elements of the Middleton's income plan must address the who as well as the how the income will be achieved. Could a spouse stay home with the kids and create a better net income by managing investments than the net income being realized by an outside job minus the income from day care? In the portion of the blog quoted, the blogger was netting only $250 after day care costs. Another blogger responded that she had become a stay-at-home mom because as a teacher making decent money, she was only taking home $200 every two weeks after deducting day care and auto costs. If she (or her spouse) could do better by staying home and using some strategy that would increase the income, would that be preferable? That is an answer that can only be determined by each family individually.

What can a family do to bring in an extra $100 a week net? A strategy like writing covered calls can bring in 3 percent or more a month and some other strategies that I regularly use myself can provide a return on risk of as much as 35 percent per month. I'll discuss strategies like spreads and condors in later chapters and give examples of some of these limited-risk, potentially high return, strategies. Suppose our struggling middle-class family could combine strategies to arrive at a level of risk acceptable to them that would return 5 percent in a month. In order to add $100 a week, they would have to work with a minimum of about $8,000 to start. Of course, with the power of compounding, that could grow rapidly. Ignoring taxes and commissions (which of course we can't in real life) just to show the power of naked compounding, starting with $8,000 and compounding at 5 percent a month would grow to more than $14,000 in a year, almost $26,000 in two years, and in a little more than four years, would have grown to more than $100,000. Which is better—making that kind of money, or accumulating $20,000 in credit card debt and paying out $4,000 a year in interest?

There are some important caveats here, of course. Just because those returns are possible does not mean it is time to quit your day job. All investing involves risk so before quitting a job and deciding to create these additional income streams, our hypothetical family and any real-life family must, yes, must understand the strategy or strategies they are going to use and they must understand the risks inherent in each such strategy. The point here is that their plan has to include provision for gaining the knowledge first and then it must incorporate practice until the strategy is well understood before ever putting any real money at risk. Only after those hurdles are cleared should any real money be put at risk. I can tell you that you can add meaningful income, but you must do the work to understand how and at what risk you can do it. Is it worth the effort? Only you can answer that question. Would you rather go through the learning curve and be able to work part-time from home and be with your kids or would you prefer to net only a $100 a week for working 40 hours at an outside job while the kids are parked at day care?

If your choice would be to work from home a couple of hours a day to net the same $100 a week or more, you'll see a number of strategies with limited risk that can enable you to achieve that goal. Condors (Chapter 6) are a lot less complicated than they may sound and provide a limited-risk vehicle where someone can generate a return on risk in the 35 percent to 40 percent a month range with no capital outlay. Selling naked puts (Chapter 7), contrary to popular belief, is a strategy that involves a lower risk than simply buying a stock yet provides a vehicle for creating regular monthly income and can be particularly useful in specific market conditions.

Naturally, some families, for reasons of their own, may decide that it is better for them if both spouses continue to work. In that event, they may still produce additional income, but may consider different strategies. They might decide to buy some closed-end funds (Chapter 3), for example, and enjoy regular dividends on a monthly or quarterly basis. These vehicles trade like stocks and have a number of advantages over the standard mutual funds. Bonds (Chapter 8), either corporate or municipal, might offer an alternative as well, or a family might utilize high-dividend-paying equities like REITs (Real Estate Investment Trusts) or MLPs (Master Limited Partnerships) to enhance income. We'll look at REITs and MLPs in Chapter 5.

As in the case of baby boomers, young families have an array of income-producing opportunities available to them. They need only make the effort to understand the vehicles they can use and then put the appropriate strategies to work for them.

YOUNG AND UNATTACHED OR NEWLY ATTACHED EXAMPLE: FORREST FOOTLOOSE

In the preceding examples, the investors had certain responsibilities and obligations arising from their status and station in life. The baby boomer example was designed to illustrate a situation where the need to preserve capital was a critical priority and generation of additional income a desirable goal. The family example demonstrates situations where added income generation is primary and maybe even necessary to help meet current living expenses as well as to position themselves for a bright financial future.

Another group, the young unattached or recently attached, will probably view income production from yet another perspective. Capital preservation is probably not as important to this group as it would be to the baby boomers and additional income may not be quite as important as it may be to a family with young children. This group may also be less risk averse than the others and, as a result may choose different strategies or a different combination of strategies. One thing that seems fairly certain is that the young are at a wonderful place to begin to create income streams that ultimately can result in great wealth. They have the advantage of added time. We saw how compounding could turn $8,000 to more than $100,000 in a little more than four years; imagine where it could take an investor writing covered calls over a 30-year period!

Once again, the starting point is the decision of how much time and effort the investor wants to devote to learning and applying strategies. Forrest Footloose, our young unattached investor, might want to devote little or no time to investment and may consider simply purchasing an annuity or annuities (Chapter 10) to create a future income stream. After letting the annuity grow over 20, 30, or 40 years, Forrest could harvest a very healthy income stream. At the opposite end of the spectrum, the young investor may decide to devote some time to study and settle on a strategy or combination of strategies that produce a current flow of additional income. The choice of strategy would be limited only by the knowledge acquired, time devoted, and initial capital available. As time passes, the income produced could be used to add to capital and produce ever-increasing streams of current and future income.

 GETTING INTO GEAR

Many of us are the same in that we each need or want more income. We would like to enjoy financial independence and have enough money to do the things we need and want to do. We would like to control more of our own time. Almost all of us could use or at least prefer to generate more income. At the same time, each of us is different. We are different ages, have different family situations, have different needs, goals, amounts of risk tolerance, amounts of money, time to devote to our investments, levels of investment knowledge, and different degrees of interest in actively creating income through investing.

Almost no matter who we are or what our individual circumstance, there are ways we can satisfy our quest for added income. The first giant step in that direction is to make the decision that we are ready and willing to go forward and do what is necessary to get the ball rolling. Making that decision is not necessarily as easy as it may sound because it requires that we commit to learning some strategies and their implementation. As strange as it sounds, it seems that most people are simply unwilling to make the decision and commit to gaining the necessary knowledge. Frankly, it isn't that difficult, but it does require devoting some time and effort. The reward can be a lifetime of higher income and the ability to enjoy many things in life that those who are unwilling to make the effort simply can never achieve. The choice is always yours and once the decision to go forward has been made, you can increase your chances of success by taking a personal inventory and then fitting a specific plan to that inventory.

Depending where you are in life, you will give greater or lesser weight to things like capital preservation. If you have no capital, there is no current reason to preserve it, but if you have accumulated a lot of capital, you probably will want your plan to emphasize protection. You probably will want to seriously consider how much time you can devote to investments and be aware of how much time you actually want to devote as well. Those are two very different things. You may have 10 hours a week that you could devote, but although you would like some extra income, you also might want to play some golf. The strategies and methods you choose can and should be tailored to your comfort level. Undoubtedly, you should also seriously consider how you deal with risk and then make the effort to choose income-producing investment strategies that fit your personal parameters. I presume that one important reason you are seeking more income is to make your life more comfortable. If that is so, I suggest you plan to use strategies and methods that fit within your comfort zone. None of this should be painful and much of it should be fun. If there is going to be any drudgery, it will be in the initial learning phase as you overcome hurdles of new concepts and particularly of new vocabulary. I can assure you, though, that the rewards that await you in terms of added income throughout your life can easily outweigh the relatively small effort you need to achieve the goal.

Once you have made the decision that you want to learn how to increase your income, you have begun the construction of an income-producing machine. Take comfort in the fact that what you are doing is for your own benefit. You are building a machine that produces income in addition to that which you earn from selling your time and efforts to an employer. It can produce that income with little time and modest effort on your part and can result in significant improvements to your lifestyle.

Just remember that if you are willing to do for six months or a year what others won't, you can do for the rest of your life what others can't.

CHAPTER 3

Assemble Your Money Machine

The Most Common Strategy of Them All

I n the field of investing, as in many other endeavors, I am a believer in understanding the basics first and only after achieving that goal, adding complexity when and where needed. In this chapter, I'll talk about the most well-known of all strategies, buy and hold. We'll look at ways both basic and obvious and maybe some not quite so basic or obvious that an investor can add some income streams to positions already held as well as ways to select new positions to enter and hold, with an important goal being the creation of additional income.

Anyone who has read my first book, *Trade Your Way to Wealth*, knows that my view of buy and hold is that there should be an answer to the question: hold until when? We'll examine some of the possible answers to that question later in this chapter, but first things first. Are you someone like my dad who was a buy-and-hold investor for many years and owned an interest in a variety of companies acquired at various times over those years? Or are you someone beginning on a path of buy-and-hold investing with an eye to the future? Depending on your answer, you will probably choose a different methodology to add to your income.

The investor who already has been holding positions in a portfolio for some time may be unlikely to be willing to part with them. If you close a position, it could mean incurring a loss or could result in a capital gain tax obligation on the profit when the position is sold and closed. An older investor once told me that he considered his positions to be old friends and he didn't want to part with them. As an aside, my dad was such an avid buy-and-hold advocate that he literally held the actual paper stock certificates in a safety deposit box. He did not part with those shares easily. No matter what the reason, even if it is purely emotional, some investors simply are not going to sell existing positions come hell or high water. Those folks are already getting whatever dividends the companies are paying and they are not going to switch into something because it happens to pay a higher dividend. They may probably have a solution by which they can add income while still holding their positions. Later in this chapter, I'll give an example of an investor who came to me with precisely that goal in mind. I'll show you what we did to substantially increase income while retaining the stock already in the portfolio.

For the new investor or someone who has already begun and is continuing to accumulate positions with a buy-and-hold strategy, we'll look at some criteria that may be useful in entering new positions and adding income at the same time. The emphasis here will be on selecting candidates that provide added income opportunities and are generally fundamentally sound so that they are the type of investment that would likely be included in a sound buy-and-hold portfolio.

The buy-and-hold investor may principally seek capital appreciation or he may focus on income production, or, maybe even more likely, a combination of the two. Whatever the case, the investor needs to ask himself some important questions. The primary step in understanding your investment personality is to ask yourself: "Why am I choosing to use the buy-and-hold approach?" There are many possible answers. It may be that is all the investor knows how to do or it could be that he has a very extended time frame and doesn't want to be bothered with the daily, weekly, or even monthly gyrations of the market. He is trying to capture capital appreciation so he should seek candidates that appear to have a high probability of growth. Certainly that is a reasonable scenario, but couldn't it even be better if our investor were able to add some substantial income along the way? Why not try to make a good thing better? We can still fulfill our primary goal of capital appreciation over time while we enjoy the benefits of more cash with only a little extra effort on our part.

In the next section, I'll begin to address the decision-making process for an investor who seeks to begin or expand a portfolio as contrasted to someone whose portfolio is already in place and who is just in the holding phase. Later in this chapter, I'll discuss some possibilities for that latter type, but, for now, we'll begin to look at ways an active investor can build a portfolio that also serves as a money machine.

NUTS AND BOLTS

As buy-and-hold investors who construct a money machine or who convert positions from stagnant to somewhat dynamic we need to make basic decisions of what categories to include and exclude in our search for appropriate candidates. The starting point, it seems to me, is to reduce the universe of potential candidates so we can decide whether to seek candidates that pay dividends, for example. If we are going to buy a stock to hold, why not include stocks that pay dividends? Obviously, if the stock pays a dividend that would add a stream of income, we could even choose to use that stream of income to buy more of the same stock through automatic dividend reinvestment.

Dividend reinvestment is a plan where the dividend you are paid is automatically used to purchase new shares at the current market price. If the company whose shares you are buying participates in such a plan, you generally pay no commission on the shares you are adding. Over time, as dividends are paid, you gain shares of stock and those added shares each will pay dividends as well.

For those reasons, at least, I would include dividend-paying stocks in the universe of possible stocks to buy. They simply add income. Would there be any reason to exclude dividend-paying stocks in deciding on the universe of stocks to search when looking for candidates to add to our portfolio? It is relatively common for newer growth stocks to pay no dividends. These companies may be using money that could otherwise be paid as dividends to shareholders to grow the company, add stores, conduct research, satisfy debt, or in some fashion improve the company. Is the lack of dividend a reason to exclude a company from consideration in a buy-and-hold portfolio? Definitely not. If capital appreciation is the primary goal, the investor may be willing to forgo receiving dividends in exchange for the chance to enjoy large gains in share price. In situations where there is no dividend, is the shareholder still able to add a stream of income? That depends on whether the stock is optionable.

If a stock is optionable (and many, if not most, are), then the investor has another avenue to generate income on his position. An option is simply a contract between two entities (people or companies) where one party to the contract pays the other party to get some right. A call contract, for example, gives the party who buys the call the right, but not the obligation, to buy a specific stock at a specific price within a specific time. In order to get that right, the call buyer pays the call seller a premium for each share covered by the contract. In turn, the call seller, because he was paid, agrees to sell shares of the specific stock to the call buyer at the agreed price (no matter what the stock is trading for on the open market) any time before the end of the agreement whenever the call buyer decides he wants to buy the stock. (For those who do not understand or trade options, I have included a detailed discussion of option basics in Appendix A.)

I'll have a lot more to say about options as I go on, but, for now, it is important to know that it can be a good thing to have the ability to trade options even if you are just a buy-and-hold investor. Since I can make income-selling calls against stock I actually own, if a stock is optionable, it gives me the chance to add to my income every month by selling those calls. It certainly makes sense, then, to include optionable stocks in the universe from which I am choosing candidates for my portfolio. The question then becomes: Should I exclude stocks that aren't optionable from my selection process? Some stocks that aren't optionable may have great potential for price appreciation (Berkshire Hathaway BRKA) comes to mind so you may not want to exclude stocks without options from your search. However, for me, in searching for buy-and-hold possibilities, I would include stocks that pay dividends or are optionable, or, preferably, both pay a dividend and are optionable. Those that pay dividends and are optionable offer multiple sources of regular income so they can have a lot to offer besides the possibility of price appreciation over time.

So, even if we consider ourselves to be buy-and-hold investors, we may be in favor of adding some income as we await price appreciation. Why not? Our search then could begin by reducing the universe of stocks we might buy to those that pay dividends, are optionable, and have a dividend reinvestment plan. That will narrow the field down considerably by culling out stocks that are not optionable and stock companies that do not pay dividends. In addition, it will present us with a situation where we will have additional streams of income from our asset. We will get dividends, we can write (sell) covered calls every month, and we will even be adding to our number of shares each time a dividend is paid and those additional shares will also pay dividends. Now we're starting to cook. Now our plan also has eliminated a fairly large number of candidates. As an aside, I should say that I have found that the way I wind up buying a particular stock is more by process of elimination than by process of selection. By deciding to buy a stock only if it pays a dividend, is optionable, and the company has a dividend reinvestment plan, I will have reduced the possibilities; and if I can continue to reduce possibilities I will wind up with a very small number of candidates that are left and that fit my objectives.

In the examples throughout the book, I have used actual numbers as of this writing. It is highly unlikely that these same conditions and pricing will exist when you read this information. These are nothing but examples designed to show the kinds of avenues that may be available over time to create income. Of course, all trading involves risk and one of the risks of any stock ownership is that the stock will decline in price and could even become worthless. The fact that a stock pays dividends, too, is no guarantee that it will continue to pay dividends.

FUEL FOR THE MONEY MACHINE: FUNDAMENTALS

The approaches in this chapter will be directed largely to the buy-and-hold investor or at least to the investor who doesn't have the time or the inclination to spend a lot of time and effort on his portfolio. However, no matter whether we are an active trader or a buy-and-hold investor we are looking for some edge to increase our odds of success. Certainly, at least for the investor with a longer time horizon, one of the important keys is sound fundamentals. When I think of fundamentals, I think of measures of a company's existence and performance that are subject to actual measurement. How much revenue did the company bring in this year compared to last? How does its debt ratio compare to other companies in the same sector? What is the current price-to-earnings ratio? What is the dividend history? The list can be very long. Fundamental analysis also can be quite complex and once analyzed the fundamentals can change quite radically and quite rapidly. However, at the same time, the fundamental information can at least give the investor some relatively current and concrete guidance about the financial health of the company. Armed with that information, the investor can at least make some educated guesses about the likelihood of future success of the company and its stock.

Fundamentals are not a panacea in my view, but are, instead, a tool for the investor. They do not always define the best candidate, but they may definitely help eliminate some prospects. Fundamental analysis also has some drawbacks. One of the chief drawbacks I have seen with investors is that there is so much information available it leads to paralysis of analysis. People can become so absorbed in attempting to find every fact in their efforts to perform due diligence that they never have enough information to pull the trigger and make the trade.

In my view, it is better to gather the limited information you, as an investor, deem most helpful and necessary to your determination and move forward. In other words, first define for yourself what elements are most important to you in assessing the financial health of a company and then see if they are present in the candidate you are considering. In the sections that follow, I'll set out some of the fundamentals that I consider to be important to me and I'll tell you why I think they are important. The list will not be all-inclusive because I use only those factors that are most important to me in making my personal decisions. You may disagree and want to look at many more (or fewer) factors. This process should become part of your investment plan. It is where you actually begin the construction of your own income machine especially if you are a buy-and-hold or long-time horizon investor.

Another thing worth mentioning before I discuss specific fundamentals is that fundamentals may help us decide what to buy but they give us little information on when to buy it. Newer investors, in particular, may fail to realize that a good company does not necessarily mean a good stock. There are many examples of great companies whose stock price languishes. E. I. DuPont de Nemours (DD), for example, may be or has been one of the greatest chemical companies ever on earth, but from 2005 to mid-2008, it channeled in about a $15 range (from a little under $40 to a little over $50) after having fallen from the $70s where it traded back in 1999. Another undeniably great company, General Electric (GE) reached a per share price in the high $50s in 2000 only to bump along in the $30s from 2004 into 2008.

Finally, always be aware that fundamentals can literally change in an instant. The next earnings report can and does often change the direction of a stock price. Litigation can drastically alter price behavior. The indictment of a CEO or CFO can devastate stock performance. New companies with new products can change industries (remember the typewriter and the record player or taking a passenger train across the country?). Even seemingly solid fundamentals can vanish through mismanagement. I don't mean to try to minimize the importance of fundamentals, I only want you to see that while they do have value they nevertheless can lull the unwary into a false sense of security.

What now follows are fundamentals that I personally think are worth examining. It isn't that any or all of them together can predict the future performance of a stock, it is just that they may give us enough of an edge to build at least a little better income generator.

General Market Conditions

Ordinarily, when we speak of fundamentals, we are examining the specifics of a particular stock, but before even doing that, we should be aware of what the market in general is doing and how the sector we are searching is performing. When we are buyers, we want to see a bullish move in our position so one of the first things I try to see is whether there is anything obvious that might impede an increase share price. In other words, what is the enemy and what pressure is it likely to bring to bear.

Little can be more formidable to bullish price movement than a bearish market. The old adage says don't try to catch a falling knife, and buying stock in a falling sector in a falling market does little to help your chances of buying a stock that is going to make a bullish move. Most stocks move in the direction of the overall market and most stocks in a sector tend to move in the direction of the sector. Picking bottoms can be a very difficult proposition. I have heard it said that a stock trader only gets one bottom and one top in his life. I've had mine, so I prefer to trade with the existing trend. If you are only going to be bullish in your trading, it is probably wise to stand aside when markets are falling and certainly when the sector in which you are interested is also dropping. Fortunately, the markets have tended to rise roughly two-thirds of the time and fall one-third so you can be planning to enter bullish positions more often than you would be standing aside and waiting your chance. Naturally, there are exceptions and one way to find them could be to search for candidates that are in rising sectors even when the markets may be falling. In any event, I believe it is important to be aware of general market conditions and sector direction before getting into the specifics of fundamental analysis of any individual equity.

Debt

When I consider what can prevent a company from succeeding or a stock price from increasing, one of the first things that comes to mind is debt. Debt can be as devastating to a company as it can be to an individual. One of the first things a financial consultant or financial planner will tell an individual is to get rid of the debt. If you are paying 20 percent or more on credit card debt, for example, you are creating a monumental hurdle to overcome before you can ever get into the black. The same principle holds true with companies. Businesses with too much debt endanger themselves. For that reason, one of the first things I look at is a company's debt/equity ratio.

The debt/equity ratio is calculated by dividing the long-term debt of a company by the common shareholders' equity. In general, the lower the number the better. Of course, some sectors naturally have a higher debt to equity ratio than others so when we look at the measure, it is important to compare the ratio to other companies in the same sector.

Airlines tend to have a very high debt to equity ratio at least in part because of the extremely high cost of their aircraft. At this writing, the major airlines generally were carrying a debt/equity of between two and three. Contrast that to an industry like oil and gas pipelines where it is not uncommon to have a ratio around one or the computer software sector where a company like Microsoft (MSFT) or BMC Software (BMC) have essentially no debt and a debt/equity ratio of zero.

Though money has been and can be made in airline stocks, I personally tend to stay away from them for several reasons. Primarily, I do not like the heavy debt and high exposure to rising fuel prices, but beyond that, I have never understood why many of the airlines can't price a seat so that they make a profit. It seems to me the airlines should be able to calculate their load rate, cost per seat mile, add a reasonable profit margin, and establish a price instead of persisting in the practice of charging differing amounts for seats on the same flight. It seems that they haven't noticed that the current pricing methods, however complex, don't seem to have worked very well as evidenced by the many airline bankruptcies over the years in addition to the severe losses many have suffered and continue to suffer.

My personal views on airlines and airline stocks aside, when looking for bullish candidates, all other things being equal, I prefer those within a given sector that have little or no debt over those that must overcome heavier burdens of debt. Again, I reiterate that by the nature of their businesses, companies in some sectors simply will have debt. The comparison that should be made, then, is to companies in the same or similar sectors and unless there is some valid and compelling reason to have a debt/equity ratio that is high and out of line with other companies in the same sector, a company with an abnormally high debt to equity ratio should be eliminated from consideration in my estimation.

Earnings

If debt is an enemy, then earnings are the ally. If I were to look at only one fundamental, it would be earnings. Typically, the term "earnings" is after-tax net income. Earnings show the profitability of a company and provide a number of useful measures. The first question is simply whether the company does have earnings. Is it profitable or not? At this point, it may be helpful to distinguish earnings from revenue. Revenue is the money a company brings in over any given period and is essentially the gross income before costs and taxes are deducted. Earnings are basically what are left after the costs and taxes are deducted from revenue. Theoretically, at least, a company can have a lot of revenue, but wind up with no earnings.

Quite often earnings are discussed in terms of earnings per share (EPS). Basically EPS is calculated by dividing the earnings by the number (or average number) of shares. EPS can then be used to calculate the familiar P/E or price-to-earnings ratio, which is simply the share price of the stock divided by the EPS. The P/E ratio can then be used to compare a stock to itself, to others in the universe of stocks, stocks in a particular index, or stocks in the same sector. As a general statement, we can see how we might be getting more value when we buy a stock with a lower P/E than with a higher P/E. It is important to understand, though, that the concept is general and in practice the statement must be carefully qualified. For the moment, it is enough to understand that if earnings stay the same and a stock price goes higher, the P/E will go higher as well. Similarly, if earnings increase but the stock price is stagnant, the P/E will be lower. One way to think about it is that P/E is telling us roughly how much we are paying to get $1 of company earnings. If a stock has a P/E of 10, for example, we are paying about $10 per share for each $1 per share the company is earning. If the stock has a P/E of 75, we are paying about $75 for each $1 per share the company is earning. At the time of this writing, Baidu.com (BIDU), a Chinese search engine company, is trading around $345 a share and the P/E is about 127. By dividing the price ($345) by the P/E (127) we can see that the EPS is a little under $3 a share. Why would we choose a stock with such a high P/E or why would we consider paying so much to "get at" one dollar of earnings? I'll discuss that shortly.

First, though, what does it mean when a stock has no P/E? It means that the company has no earnings; it is not profitable. The stock of many companies soared during the Internet or tech bubble in the late 1990s. Stocks with no P/E or with astoundingly high P/Es were abundant and prices continued to rise until the bubble ultimately burst. Why the phenomena occurred and why one would even consider buying a stock with a very high P/E have the same answer. Speculators were betting that the companies would become profitable or, if already profitable, that earnings would increase substantially. Naturally, if earnings were to increase dramatically, the E part of the P/E equation would be higher and presumably the P/E would fall more into line with traditional concepts. The bubble burst when it became clear that many of the high-flyers would never have earnings or at least great earnings just because they had some Internet-related business plan. The no-hopers fell by the wayside and the whole market corrected from this mammoth miscalculation. Meanwhile, though, some companies like BIDU still have high P/Es years later as I write this chapter. Is the same mistake being repeated? Only time can answer that question, but there is logic to the concept that a company like BIDU will have increased earnings. The company is important in the Chinese market and that market is just beginning to be tapped. The Internet in China is exploding and BIDU is an early and profitable player. Those buying BIDU shares may well discount the high P/E with the belief that earnings will increase as the Chinese population comes on board the Internet.

As we have seen, EPS and P/E are helpful measures in determining the financial health of a company. How can we use these measures to help guide us to specific investments? First, I would ordinarily prefer a company with earnings over a company that is not profitable. Then, I like to compare the earnings of the company I am examining to its past EPS. I am looking to see earnings growth year over year. Again, unless there is some good explanation for the drop, I am likely to eliminate a company that has declining EPS from further consideration. I also want to compare the EPS of the current quarters to the same quarters in the past. This approach helps paint a picture of the progress or lack thereof that a company is experiencing. I also suggest seeing how the P/E of a company compares to other companies in the same sector. If it seems out of line, I look to see whether there is an apparent reason. Is the P/E exceptionally high for the sector? If so, is it because the stock price has climbed or is it because earnings are down? If because earnings are down, why have they fallen? Has the company engaged in plant expansion, for example, or are sales and revenue just down?

Bottom line, for me, is whether the P/E seems to be in a reasonable range for the index in which the stock trades and particularly within its own sector, and have EPS been increasing year over year and with respect to the same quarters the previous year.

Usually, it takes less time to make those assessments than it probably takes to read this section, but the relatively little time spent can definitely help understand a company's financial health and give some information as to the likelihood of future performance.

Dividends

We are trying to assemble the parts to build our money machine, so we would be remiss to overlook the importance of dividends in our exploration of fundamentals. The basic question is whether the company has been paying dividends, but it is probably a good idea to expand the search a bit further. Answers to questions like how often is the dividend paid, what is the yield, what is the payment history, and what is the history of increasing dividends all may add to the edge we are seeking.

Later in this chapter, I will touch on certain types of investments like MLPs that often pay high dividends. I'll look at them again along with certain closed-end funds in Chapter 5 when I'll discuss trading high-dividend stocks to capital gains as well as dividends by actively trading these issues. For now, we need only be aware that some classes of investments tend to supply higher yields than most other stocks.

Beyond the yield, alone, I also look for companies whose dividends have a history of growth. A number of companies have a history of raising their dividends every year or at least with some degree of regularity. Dividend growth is a practice that can be very beneficial. When a company increases its dividend, obviously, the investor is paid more in dividends but also the increasing dividends will help move the stock price up as well. In general, the more income a company produces (and dividends are usually paid from income) the more valuable its stock will become. Since increasing dividends are likely to result from increasing income or EPS, there is an incentive for buyers to pay a higher price for the stock. One way I use to find those companies that do grow their dividends is a search on one of my favorite software programs. Worden Brothers, who created and market some excellent charting services, include a sort based on dividend growth rate over a five-year period in their *Telechart*® programs and, in their most recent release, *Blocks*™, also provide an easy way to sort for companies with growing dividends in the universe of stocks or any subuniverse.

One other consideration worth mentioning is the possibility of dividend reinvestment. Some companies offer a plan where the investor can choose to receive his dividends in the form of stock rather than as cash (DRIP). These plans usually offer a free stock purchase plan (SPP) where the enrollee can make periodic purchases of company stock with no (or at least low) fees or commissions. Though the dividends are still taxed, the plan has the advantage of providing a cost-effective way of adding shares while at the same time dollar-cost averaging. Dollar-cost averaging is simply a method by which more shares are purchased when the price per share is lower and fewer shares are purchased when the price is higher.

An awareness of a company's history and practice regarding the payment of dividends and increases to dividends can be helpful in selecting candidates for a portfolio where the investor's goals include the production of regular income in addition to the possibility of growth over time.

PEG Ratio

Another measure that can tell us a great deal about a company is the PEG (price earnings to growth) ratio. This ratio is calculated by dividing the price/earnings ratio we discussed earlier by the year over year earnings growth rate. Here, again, a lower number would ordinarily be preferable to a higher number. If the P/E was 20, for example, and the company's earnings were growing at a 10 percent per year rate, the PEG would be 2. Contrast that situation where the same 20 P/E exists, but the earnings growth rate was only 2 percent a year. In that latter case, the PEG would be a much higher 10.

On the other hand, if we were to compare two companies, both of which had a year over year growth rate of 5 percent, but one had a P/E of 15 and the other a P/E of 50, the PEGs would be 3 and 10, respectively. I don't know about you, but all other things being equal, I'd be more likely to go for the stock with the lower P/E and, therefore, lower PEG.

Return on Equity

Here, again, is an excellent measure for comparing the profitability of a company to other companies in the same industry or sector. In essence, the return on equity (ROE) is the measure of profitability that a company achieves with the money shareholders have invested. It is calculated by dividing net income by shareholder equity. In the case of ROE, the higher the number, the better the return so I prefer those companies in a sector that attains the higher returns on equity.

Price-to-Book Value Ratio

Another fundamental I like to check is the price-to-book value ratio, commonly called price-to-book. The book value of a company is the accounting value of the company. Though book value can be relatively complex, for my purposes, I think of it as the net asset value of a company or the breakup value of the company. In other words, what's it worth if we had to sell it today. The price-to-book is calculated by dividing the share price by the book value per share. If the book value of a company is $25 a share and the stock price is $25 a share, the price-to-book would be 1. At times, the share price of stock in a company will be less than the breakup value, in which case there may be theoretically less risk than there would be in a company whose share price is some high multiple of the book value. That information, alone, is not enough for me to make any final decision about including a stock in my own portfolio. It is just another factor to be considered in the overall mix and, for me, is less important than considerations of debt and earnings.

As in the case of other fundamentals, the ratio can be helpful in comparing stocks within the same sector or industry. As an example, as of the time I am writing this section, I checked the price-to-book of some investment brokerages and found that Ameritrade (AMTD) had a price-to-book of 4.2 and Charles Schwab (SCHW) had a price-to-book of 7.2 while Goldman Sachs (GS) came in at 1.77. By themselves, these price-to-book ratios would probably not lead us to choose or reject any of those companies as investments. The relative numbers, though, in combination with other fundamentals discussed here can help us narrow the field and ultimately arrive at a choice to include as part of the money machine we are constructing.

SOME HELP FROM SECTORS: UTILITIES

Another place to look for income possibilities is within sectors of the market. Some types of companies tend to pay better dividends than others. I remember parents and grandparents talking about stock dividends and how great the telephone and electric companies were because they were safe investments that faithfully paid good dividends. They were talking about utility companies. Even today, many utility companies pay excellent dividends, and though they may not be exciting, can provide relatively stable platforms for income production.

Electric Utilities

As I write this section, of the more than 50 electric utility or electric holding companies, at least 30 pay a dividend and have options available on their stock (Appendix B). While a few pay small dividends, most seem to pay between about 2.5 percent to about 6 percent with the majority clustered between 3 percent and 5 percent.

Otter Tail Corporation (OTTR), as an example, is trading near $37 a share as I write this section and at that price, the dividend yield based on payment history is about 3.2 percent annually. Also, at this time, selling the one month out $40 calls every month would generate a premium of about 1 percent per month. If we assumed all things would remain equal (which of course they wouldn't) someone who owned 1,000 shares of OTTR could expect to bring in about $1,200 a year in dividends and another $3,500 to $4,500 selling out-of-the-money calls. Five thousand a year on a $37,000 investment is about a 13.5 percent return on the investment even if the stock does nothing. The investor doesn't need to do anything after he has bought the stock to get the $1,200 in dividends and once he gets the hang of it, he will probably spend 15 minutes or so a month selecting calls to sell to bring in the other $4,000 for the year. To look at it another way, it works out to be about $1,733 an hour for time expended on the strategy in that example. While this specific play may not be available by the time you read this book, you probably will be able to find comparable possibilities. In any event, the example shows how some significant income can be obtained with relatively little effort to someone willing to make the effort.

Just to illustrate a slightly different approach to reach similar ends, Duke Energy (DUK) was trading around $18.60 and paying an annual dividend of about 4.7 percent. We could buy about twice as many shares of DUK as of this writing as we could of OTTR. With 2,000 shares of DUK, we could expect to receive about $1,750 in dividends. Though DUK does have options, they are not too actively traded and the premiums are not spectacular. In this case, instead of selling calls each month, we might decide to sell them only a couple of times a year. As I write, I see I could sell the $20 strike with a five-month out expiration for 40 cents a share. If I did that, I would bring in $800 twice a year or $,1600. Since I would only have to make a decision a couple of times a year, my total time on this buy and hold example might be an hour for the year. Again, if we looked at this as how much we were earning per hour of effort, it would work out to about $3,300 an hour. Of course, if we got called out of our DUK for $20, we would make $1.40 a share plus whatever dividends we had already received plus the premium we got for the call. Suppose we got one dividend ($440), one premium of $800, and the stock was called away from us for a

$1.40 a share or $2,800 profit. Not bad, either. We would have made $4,040 less the commissions. Only you can decide whether that is good or bad.

Gas Utilities

Many of the same things that are true of electric utilities are true of gas utilities as well. When selecting any utility, the investor may also have a preference for one type over the other. If the investor has some reason to believe, for example, that the supply of or demand for natural gas will cause the price to rise, he may decide that the share price of natural gas utilities may grow faster than the price of electric utilities or vice versa and may decide to invest in one over the other recognizing that each will provide candidates that both pay dividends and are optionable.

Equitable Resources (EQT) is a fairly expensive stock. While trading near $75 a share, its dividend yield was only on the order of 1.2 percent. The company has been paying 22 cents per share per quarter so just looking at the dividend alone without regard to potential price appreciation I would not be hysterically excited about the opportunity for income. However, I also saw that I could sell the next strike price up call ($80) with 30 days remaining to expiration for about $1 a share. For those who may not be familiar with call options, that means someone would pay me $1 a share for the right to buy my stock—for which we'll assume I paid $75 a share—for $80 a share anytime before the option expires, which in this case is 30 days away. No matter what, I get to keep the $1 a share. Obviously, no one would buy my stock for $80 if they could get it cheaper on the open market, so if the 30 days passed and the stock wasn't above $80, I would still have my stock and the extra $1 a share. I could do it all over the next month and the next and the next. . . . You get the picture. Of course, if the stock was above $80 a share someone would buy it at the $80 mark and I would have another $5 a share profit. In other words, it looks like I can generate about 1.3 percent a month selling one strike out-of-the-money calls in addition to collecting the dividend. On an annual basis, I could collect the dividend and sell one strike out-of-the-money calls every month and enjoy a return in the 16 percent to 17 percent range for not much effort. Of course, whenever I sell a call, there is the possibility that my stock will be called and I'll have to sell it at the strike price.

If I were to be called out under the facts of this example, I would make an additional 6.7 percent, but of course I would not have the stock any longer. The idea that their stock has been sold bothers many people, but in most cases, I have no idea why. If they are selling out-of-the-money calls and they are called out, that means they made a profit. What is wrong with making a profit? Maybe it is just me, but I think a profit is a good thing. "Yes, but I have to pay taxes," is often the wail. True, taxes must be paid, but only on the gain and if it happens to be a long-term gain, the taxes (as of this writing) are at a much reduced level. Please keep in mind, though, that even if the stock gets called away, nothing prevents me from just buying more shares. If I really like the company, I could wait for a dip and buy more shares or I could buy shares right after mine were called away and just continue the process. Having stock called away when an option is exercised is usually not a bad thing. If you have sold out-of-the-money calls, you have made a profit on the shares, themselves, and you keep the premium for the calls you sold.

MASTER LIMITED PARTNERSHIPS

Though Master Limited Partnerships (MLPs) are technically different from many traded companies, they still trade just like a stock and many have options available as well. These entities are not corporations; they are partnerships that are publicly traded. MLPs are restricted to certain businesses, notably those engaged in oil and gas extraction and in the transportation of those commodities through things like pipelines or ships.

One of the desirable qualities of MLPs is that they are required to make distributions to the investors and these tend to be relatively attractive. Since these are partnerships rather than corporations, they are not burdened with corporate income taxes, which, undoubtedly, help to achieve a better return to investors. In Appendix B, I have listed a number of MLPs and the dividend yield of each as of this writing. The yield ranged from approximately 5 percent to 9 percent per year.

Though I do not profess to be a tax expert, and urge you to consult a competent tax professional before acting on anything financial, I understand that investors are able to deduct their pro rata share of the MLPs depreciation on their tax returns' personal returns.

In addition to those benefits, a number of the MLPs are also optionable so an investor can also sell calls against his position and enjoy the possibility of even more income on top of the dividend and tax benefits.

As is the case with any stock, MLPs also have risk. There is always the risk that Congress may decide it wants more of your money and may change the tax laws, removing some or all the tax advantages of an MLP. As with stocks, the share price of MLPs can fluctuate fairly significantly though, in general, the beta (tendency to respond to swings in the market) for MLPs tends to be relatively low. For example, a beta of 1 essentially suggests a security's price will move with the market while a beta of less than 1 would suggest that the price would be less volatile than the market overall. In looking at the selection of MLPs listed in Appendix B, the beta of all but two is well below 1 with the lowest at the time of writing being less than 0.1. This information suggests that there may be less risk as well as the possibility of a lesser reward in terms of share price. In other words, I would normally not expect wild price gyrations in these investments. However, we must always be aware that there can be exceptions and the price of any MLP could drop significantly from our purchase price and result in a loss.

Something worth keeping in mind with investments such as MLPs where there is a relatively high yield is a point made to me a few years ago by an astute broker with whom I deal. The message is particularly appropriate where, as in this chapter, an investor may be considering the generation of income from a buy-and-hold strategy. The point is that the return on our investment remains the same as long as we hold the position and the dividend doesn't change. Suppose I bought an investment for $10 a share and it paid a dividend of $1 a share. The yield on my investment would be 10 percent, wouldn't it? Since I invested $10, as long as the dividend remained $1 a share, my return on investment would be 10 percent no matter where the share price went. If I bought 1,000 shares of XYZ at $10 and paid $10,000, I would get $1,000 a year in dividends. My investment is $10,000, my return is $1,000. If the stock price went to $12 a share, my investment was still $10,000 and my return still $1,000; if the price dipped to $8 a share, my investment was still $10,000 and the return still 10 percent of that investment. When income is the paramount consideration and we achieve a satisfactory return on our investment, we may not need to be as concerned by fluctuations in price as we might if we were a more active trader.

The same principle applies even when we are selling covered calls as I'll discuss in Chapter 4. If I bought XYZ at $10 a share and sold a specific call at 40 cents a share, I can often adjust the strike price I sell month after month as the stock price moves up and down so that I still bring in about the same 40 cents a share every month. It won't be exactly the same every month, but I will still be able to sell a call that approximates the same return on investment with some regularity.

 GETTING INTO GEAR

In this chapter, we looked at ways to build our money machine using the most common and well-known strategy of them all—buy and hold. We have explored the use of particular vehicles like utilities, REITs, and MLPs to garner higher income through higher dividends, and we have looked at optionable stocks to begin our understanding of how we can add regular monthly income to already existing positions as well to ones we are newly acquiring.

Next, we considered fueling our machine. By fueling, I mean choosing specific investments to create our money machine. We saw the important influence general market conditions have on the direction of individual stock prices. This understanding can help us stand aside when markets are moving in the "wrong" direction and give us an edge when entering new positions.

We have also explored some of the fundamentals to which an investor might look when selecting candidates for a portfolio. These fundamentals provide information to help us get a little edge in building our money machine. We have seen things like heavy debt that can impede corporate profits, but we have also learned to compare apples to apples and understand that when we look at debt/equity ratios we should be comparing them to companies in the same industry. We have also looked at the importance of earnings, PEG, and ROE as indicators of financial health of a company and factors that are likely to influence the price movement of its shares.

As we go forward, I'll address the implementation of income-producing strategies beyond simple buy and hold. In the next chapter, I'll discuss writing covered calls in much greater depth and not only expand on how the buy-and-hold investor can use his portfolio to make additional monthly income, but also we'll look at some ways that writing covered calls can be used to reduce risk and yield a decent percentage return on a regular basis.

Interchangeable Parts for the Money Machine

The chapters that follow explore a number of specific strategies that range from writing covered calls to selling naked puts, from bonds to reverse mortgages, and lots in between. We'll see where risks lie, and what potential reward each strategy offers. We'll examine precise ways to enter, use, and exit these money-making strategies. Using our hypothetical characters from Part I—the Baldings, the Middletons, and Forrest Footloose—we'll look at various examples to illustrate different approaches and ways to add parts to our money machines.

Each chapter is specifically designed to address potential uses of a specific strategy. As the reader explores these possibilities, I would suggest he consider how the strategy might fit his own needs. Are the risks within his tolerance, for example? How active does an investor or trader need to be in monitoring any particular strategy and how much time does he have to devote to active management of the strategy? What will the strategy do for him in both the long run and the short run? How complex does the strategy seem to be? Is the trader willing to take the time to understand the particular strategy?

Recognizing that some strategies will offer higher potential rewards and that some strategies will require less time or involve less risk, the reader should look for a balance that will leave him content. In my view, he should choose strategies that have a risk level compatible with enjoying a good night's sleep every night. If he has little time to devote to monitoring positions, he should choose strategies that require little time. If he is new to investing, the reader should probably select less complex strategies at first and move to more complex only after he has added knowledge.

As with so much of life, investment decisions often can go much better if combined with common sense. If you can't swim, it probably isn't a good idea to dive into water that you know is over your head. In investing, even though some other strategy may offer a higher potential reward, it is undoubtedly better to go with the strategy you know well as opposed to the one that you don't know so well but which might lead to a higher return. In essence, I'm suggesting the crawl before you walk approach. I have seen all too many fall flat on their faces using the ready, fire, aim approach.

Each of the strategies that follow can provide added income and can be an effective part of your money machine so even if you start by crawling, you will still be advancing; you will still be creating a machine that pays you. As you go from crawling to walking, you may add strategies you find in the next chapters to charge up the production from your money machine. Indeed, you may find that you are combining some basic strategies to reduce risk and turbocharge your machine. Whatever you decide, make it comfortable for yourself and know that without much effort, you are doing what so many others aren't. You are building a machine that pays you money.

CHAPTER 4

The Call That Pays You

A Variety of Ways to Ring Up Cash

I n Chapter 3 I introduced the concept of selling calls against stocks in a buy-and-hold portfolio. In this chapter, I'll expand on that strategy and discuss a number of ways an investor can write covered calls to generate regular income either as part of a larger strategy such as buy and hold or as a strategy in and of itself. For readers who may be completely unfamiliar with stock options and option trading I have set out the basics in Appendix A. Now would be a good time to read that information before proceeding any further unless you already know what an option is and are familiar with the terminology such as strike prices, premiums, and expirations. If you already have an understanding of the basics, you are ready to proceed.

EXACTLY WHAT WRITING A COVERED CALL MEANS

Just as a little review: A call option is a contract where the buyer of the call obtains the right but does not have the obligation to buy the stock at the strike price anytime before expiration (in the case of American-style options) and, to obtain the right, pays the seller of the call a premium. The seller of the call, on the other hand, is paid a premium to undertake the obligation to deliver the stock to the call buyer at the strike price anytime before expiration if the call buyer "calls" or exercises his option. Basically, that's it. The buyer pays a per share premium to get the right to buy stock at a certain price within a specific time and the seller agrees to deliver stock at that same price if the option is exercised.

The term "writing," in stock market lingo, simply means selling. So when we say we are writing calls, all we mean is that we are selling calls. "Covered" means we own the underlying or already own the stock on which we are selling the calls. If we sold calls without owning the stock first, that would be called writing naked calls since we would not have any stock to sell at the time. Naked writing is a totally separate strategy and high-risk strategy that is not part of this discussion.

Here we will examine various ways an investor can use covered calls to create added income. Regardless of your investment preferences, if you include stock ownership in your arsenal of strategies, some knowledge of ways to use covered calls to enhance cash flow will probably be helpful.

GREAT THINGS WRITING COVERED CALLS CAN DO FOR YOU

As a result of the generation of additional regular income, covered calls have the added advantage of reducing the risk in the underlying stock position. Obviously, if you own shares of stock, your risk is whatever you paid to buy the stock. Though it thankfully is not a regular occurrence, companies do disappear and the stock price can literally go to zero so an investor can lose his total investment. However, if the investor owns stock and sells covered calls against his position, the overall risk is reduced by whatever premium is received. If an investor bought XYZ shares for $50, the initial risk (ignoring commissions) would be $50. However, if he sold the $55 calls for $1, the risk would now only be $49 ($50 a share less the $1 premium received for selling the call). If the process is repeated over time, the total dollar risk in the underlying stock position becomes less and less when each premium is received. The trade-off for this income and reduction in risk is that the topside is capped absent any other action by the investor. If he sold the $55 call and the stock went to $70 a share without any other action by the investor, he would be called out of his position and would be required to sell his shares for $55. He would keep the premium for the calls he sold and would sell the stock for a $5 a share profit, but he would not get the extra $15 a share for which the stock might be trading. His profit would be capped at the $55 price. Many investors refuse to write covered calls because of this kind of possibility and that becomes a personal choice. When I use the writing covered call strategy, I do not mind capping the upside. Yes, occasionally, I will miss a run-up, but I find that isn't a bad trade-off for a regular 2 percent or 5 percent a month return on my investment.

WAYS COVERED CALLS CAN BENEFIT DIFFERENT INVESTORS

In the remainder of this chapter, I'll describe a number of ways in which covered calls can be written. We'll start by looking at the situation where the investor is of the buy-and-hold variety and does not want his stock called away no matter what, but still wouldn't mind a little extra income. Next, we'll examine several ways in which the investor can use writing covered calls as a specific income-producing strategy where one goal might actually be to be called out of positions each month. Finally, we'll see a way in which to exercise even greater leverage by selling calls against other options in order to reduce the dollar risk and, at the same time, increase the percentage return. Each of these approaches can produce a stream of income. You will be able to decide whether any one or combination suits your trading personality and helps achieve your goals.

THE BALDING FAMILY: I WANT TO KEEP MY STOCK BUT STILL MAKE INCOME

You may recall this hypothetical family from Chapter 2. Ed Balding has reached retirement age and he and his wife, Grace, have two grown children and three grandkids. Their house is paid for and Ed gets a little pension from the company where he worked and is eligible for Social Security retirement benefits. Ed had been employed by TellyPhone,[*] a company in the communications industry, for many years and had accumulated 2,500 shares of TellyPhone stock over that time. In addition, the Baldings have another $500,000 in liquid assets accumulated from the sale of a rental property and some savings. Ed is very loyal to his old employer and has no intention of selling his stock.

Considering all that information, it doesn't sound like the Baldings are too badly off, but they have a lot of life left and are on a fixed income. What might they consider doing? As far as the TellyPhone stock, at least, the Baldings are definite buy-and-hold investors. However, the stock price has dropped almost 20 percent in the last month, and the company is facing some tough challenges from competitors. Why not at least try to make some added income from that asset even if the goal is not to sell the stock?

---

[*]The companies for whom hypothetical characters in this book worked are fictional, but the stock prices and option prices used in the various examples are based on actual prices for existing companies in the same industry as the fictional company as of the time this is written.

Currently, the stock is trading around $32.50 a share so the Baldings have an asset worth $81,250. The $35 calls that expire in a little over a month could be sold for about $0.50 a share. That means that the Baldings could sell 25 contracts (2,500 shares ÷ 100 shares per contract) of the $35 calls that expire in five weeks and bring in $1,250 before a commission for that five-week period. That is a five-week return of 1.5 percent. If the Baldings could repeat that every five weeks (and they could probably do that or pretty close to that) 10 times during the year, they would add nearly $12,500 to their annual income. Can that kind of added income help? I would guess that an additional $12,500 in income a year might be greatly appreciated by the Baldings as well as many others.

Risks of Covered Call Writing

Value of the Stock   What are the risks to the Baldings? The first risk is the value of the stock. Anytime we own stock without doing anything else, our risk is equal to the price of the stock. The stock price could literally go to zero and while that may be unlikely, it is much more likely than most investors may think. Consider all the dot-com stocks that went belly up when the tech bubble burst, think about companies like Enron. Has anyone flown on Eastern Airlines recently? In the Baldings' case, before selling calls against their TellyPhone position, their risk is $81,250. After they sell calls the first time, the risk drops to $80,000, and assuming a stagnant stock price, after about a year of selling those calls, the risk is down to about $68,750.

Emotional Ownership   There are, of course, the additional risks of having to sell the stock if called out and of possible lost opportunity. Remember, Mr. Balding is wed to his stock by emotion and doesn't want it sold even if selling it would mean taking even more profit. My advice to Mr. Balding in that scenario is: "Get over it." Even if the stock went above $35 and it was assigned (the 35 call exercised and the stock called away), Mr. Balding would make an additional $6,250 because he would be selling the stock for $2.50 a share more than it was trading when he sold the calls. In situations like this, I've heard investors say, "I don't care how much I get; I just want to keep my stock." These folks seem to forget that they can always buy the stock again. Once a stock is sold there is no law against buying it again. In a moment, I'll discuss ways to avoid being called out, but first I want to address the other risk of lost opportunity.

Loss of Opportunity   One admitted downside of selling covered calls is that the stock price may soar and the stock could be called at a lower price than it is trading at the market. Suppose Mr. Balding did sell the $35 calls at 50 cents when the stock was trading around $32.50 and then the stock jumped to $40 and before Mr. Balding did anything else his shares were called away. Well, he would have made the 50 cents a share he got when he sold the calls and he would enjoy an additional $2.50 a share profit over the price it was when he sold the calls. On the other hand, he would have missed the additional $5 the stock moved. If that is a problem (and I don't think it should be), the answer is either do not sell covered calls or, if the stock price reaches a level where the call could be assigned, close the call by buying it back or roll the call up and out by simultaneously buying to close the original call (which may result in a loss on that call) and selling a higher strike the next month out. For example, in our hypothetical, Mr. Balding owns the stock at $32.50 and sells the $35 call with expiration five weeks away for 50 cents. Suppose four weeks pass and the stock price jumps to $36. Now those $35 calls will have a week until they expire but are now $1 in the money and still have a week of time value so they now may be worth $1.25 a share. Mr. Balding could buy to close his $35 calls and would lose $0.75 a share on the call transactions, *but* notice that the stock price rose $3.50, more than making up for the loss on the calls.

Instead of just buying back those $35 calls, Mr. Balding might also look at the option chain for the next month expiration and find that he could sell the $40 calls for that expiration at $0.60. Now, instead of losing 75 cents on the options, he would have lost only 15 cents on the options and gained $3.50 in share price. Now, if he were called out at $40 after another jump in price, he would have $7.50 a share profit in the stock.

The bottom line is that the Baldings need not have their stock assigned if that is a truly significant priority and can avoid assignment by buying back or buying to close any options they sold or by rolling the calls out to a later expiration or out and up to a higher strike. Naturally, if the actual stock price does not reach or exceed the strike price they sold, they just keep the money they got for selling the calls and keep repeating the process month after month.

Managing Time Spent Monitoring Covered Calls

Though it may sound like a lot of effort to sell calls each month and keep an eye on stock prices, it really isn't and is an awfully good trade-off of time spent versus return achieved as far as I am concerned. However, if Ed Balding just can't be bothered with looking at these positions a couple of times a month, he could choose to sell a further out expiration rather than a nearer term and he could have chosen to sell a higher strike as well. In the case of TellyPhone, Ed might choose to sell the same $35 call, but with an expiration about six months away rather than five weeks away. Since one of the significant elements in option pricing is time value and Ed is selling time, we would expect the premium for a call that expires in six months to be greater than the premium only a few weeks away for the same strike price. In this case, the $35 call with the expiration a little more than six months away could be sold for about $1.65 a share. If Ed chose to sell those calls, he would bring in about $6,625 before commission or a half-year return of roughly 5 percent. That return would still be a nice addition to income and Ed wouldn't have to look at the position quite so often.

Yet another alternative requiring even less monitoring would be to sell even longer-term calls. TellyPhone, for example, has LEAPS® (long-term equity anticipation securities) that trade just like options but have expirations that are sometimes as far out as three years. In this case, Ed and Grace could choose to sell the $35 calls expiring in about a year and a half for about $3.20 a share to bring in a tidy $8,000 before commissions. Instead of selling the $35 calls, they could consider selling an even higher strike giving the shares more room to move up before being in a position where they might be called. Selling the year and a half out $40 calls, for example, would bring in about $1.75 a share.

When Will Stock Be Called (Assigned)?   For those who may be new to writing covered calls or options in general, I should note that when a trader or investor sells a call, it does not necessarily mean that their stock will be called away immediately just because the stock price goes above the strike price sometime before expiration. With American-style options, the owner of a call may exercise his option *anytime* before expiration. However, practicality dictates that unless the option is deep in the money early exercise is relatively uncommon. As long as the option is out of the money—the strike price is higher than the current stock price—there would be no reason to exercise. The call buyer could buy the stock at a lower price on the open market than he could by exercising his option so there is no point to exercising the call. Even if the call is in the money with time left before expiration, the call buyer is more likely to just sell his call than he would be to exercise his option and buy the stock.

Option premiums consist of both intrinsic and time value. If the strike price is at or above the stock price, the option has no intrinsic value, only time value. However, if the option strike is in the money, the premium consists of both intrinsic and time value. If a stock is trading at $37 and we own the $35 calls, we are in the money and we know that the $35 call has an intrinsic value of $2, but, with time left until expiration, it also has some time value. If the time value is $0.50 then the whole premium would be $2.50. With the stock trading at $37, is the holder of the $35 calls with a premium of $2.50 better off exercising his option and buying the stock at $35 or is he better off selling his option for $2.50? If he exercises his calls and buys the stock he will have to come up with $35 a share to buy the stock (or at least half that on margin) at that price. Suppose he holds 10 contracts controlling 1,000 shares, then he can buy the stock for $35,000 and turn around and sell it for $37,000—chalking up a $2,000 gain. On the other hand, if he just sells his 10 contracts at $2.50, he'll have $2,500 instead. It's easy to see that it is better for the call owner to just sell his calls in this situation than to exercise the option and buy the stock.

Once I've Sold a Call, Am I Stuck with the Position Until Expiration? Another thing to keep in mind is that just because someone sells a covered call does not mean that the position must stay open until the option expires. Many times in my own trading I will sell an option at what I believe is a relatively high price with the intent of closing the position when the premium falls. In such cases, I am selling high and buying low (it's the same as buying low and selling high, only the order in which you do it is reversed; that is, first you sell high and later buy low). When we write a covered call, we sell to open the position. We do the opposite—buy to close if we want to exit the same position. As an example, if we are selling time value (and that is exactly what we are selling when we sell at- or out-of-the-money calls), in general, we can expect the time value to decrease as time passes. All other things being equal, when there is less time remaining, there is less value. If we have sold time and some time passes, the premium for time value has diminished and we could buy to close our position for less than we sold it in the first place.

What might the Baldings do to generate income with the rest of their assets? We'll look at many other possibilities in later chapters, but they may also choose to adopt some of the strategies the Middletons and Forrest Footloose consider in the following sections.

THE MIDDLETONS: STRATEGY FOR AN IRA OR ROTH IRA

As you may recall from Chapter 2, the hypothetical Middleton family have a much different perspective from the Baldings. Tim and Mary are up to their ears in debt, are both working to make ends meet, and are raising children so they have added expenses associated with day care. They have been contributing to a Roth IRA with $10,000 in it and have about $3,000 in savings. Can a covered call strategy help them? As always, the answer is partially dependent on how much time they may be willing or able to devote to a strategy. They do have a great opportunity with their Roth IRA.

Selling covered calls in the Roth could ultimately result in quite a nice treasure chest over time.

Using ETFs (Exchange-Traded Funds)

One thing the Middletons may want to consider is trading a whole market or a sector rather than individual stocks. Whole markets are not as likely to react to many risks that would injure individual stocks. A company can have many things happen that could really hurt its stock price. It could go bankrupt, become the defendant in serious litigation, have an officer arrested, suffer an earnings setback, or any number of other things that would result in a sharp drop in price. While such events could devastate a particular stock, they likely would have little or no effect on the overall market.

Trading whole markets can be accomplished using Exchange-Traded Funds (ETFs) that also have options. ETFs have some distinct qualities in that they can be traded just like stocks, have very low fees, permit an investor to trade a basket of stocks instead of an individual issue, and often are optionable. The Powershares QQQ Trust (QQQQ) is the NASDAQ 100 Index Tracking Stock and enables an investor to trade an equivalent of the NASDAQ 100 in a single stock. It is heavily traded and has options. Since markets have gone up over time, the Middletons may want to buy shares in QQQQ as a vehicle for potential growth and a position against which they could sell covered calls in their Roth. Other whole market ETFs such as the Diamonds (DIA) representing the Dow 30 Industrials and the Spyders (SPY) that represent the S&P 500 are also available.

If Tim and Mary decided to buy shares of QQQQ in their Roth on the day I am writing this section, they would be paying $44.64 a share. They could immediately sell the $45 calls that expire less than a month and a half from now and would receive $1.60 a share. Before commission, that is a return of more than 3.5 percent in 41 days. Disregarding commissions for the purposes of this example, if the Middletons were to sell these calls every month and a half and get approximately the same 3.5 percent each time, their $10,000 would turn into $13,168 or a return for the year of better than 31 percent. That compounding with no taxation can really grow money quickly. Even if the Middletons could get only 2 percent per month, the original $10,000 could grow to almost $33,000 in five years without any additional contributions.

Since time is always an issue and the Middletons have little extra, they might consider selling a call with expiration a full year away rather than selling calls every month or six weeks. In that case, they would free up a little time, but would enjoy a less spectacular result. The $45 calls expiring a year away are selling for $5.05 a share or slightly better than an 11 percent return. While that is a far cry from the 31 percent they might make selling the options each month and a half, 11 percent is still not a terrible return. In 10 years at that rate, for example, the original $10,000 would turn into almost $35,000 and in 20 years could top the $120,000 mark.

Now the Middletons have a plan that can help move their Roth in the right direction. In each of the examples, you may have noticed that we have looked at selling at- or near-the-money calls. The reason for that is because I want to get the biggest bang for my buck in time value and the greatest premium for time value is in the at-the-money options. As we sell further out-of-the-money options, the premium for time is less because it is less likely that the stock price will reach the strike price by expiration than it is with at-the-money options, which have a strike close to the current stock price. In the case of in-the-money options that have intrinsic value in addition to time value, the time value portion is also less than the time value of at-the-money options. Selling the at-the-money calls, then, provides the greatest return in terms of time value.

The Middletons may like and adopt the writing covered call strategy in their Roth IRA, but because of the limitations against taking money out of the IRA, they are still confronted with the need for present income they can use to help pay the monthly bills.

Classic Covered Call Strategies

So far, we've looked at various selections we might make when writing covered calls. Depending on our personal goals and constraints, we might choose to sell longer or shorter expirations; we might decide to sell in-the-money, at-the-money, or out-of-the-money calls. We can use these methods to create regular current income, or we might want to employ them in a tax-advantaged account. The sections that follow will outline important considerations for an investor who engages in writing covered calls.

Look for Bullish Candidates   One way the Middletons might consider adding a stream of income is to employ a classic covered call strategy. By that, I mean selecting a stock, a time frame, and a return that will generate income on a monthly basis. In general, selling covered calls is a bullish strategy. If we own a stock, whether we are selling covered calls or not, we do not want the price to go down. We want the price to go up or at least stay the same. Since stock ownership is part of the covered call writing strategy, we want to choose stocks that look bullish. One way to find candidates is to look for leading stocks in sectors that are moving up, especially in markets that are moving up. Unfortunately, many new covered call writers find candidates where the premium for calls is high, but the stock price is falling. Once the stock price falls below the price you paid for it minus what the market paid you for selling a call, you are in a losing position and that is something we try to avoid by choosing bullish candidates.

Limit the Price to Pay for the Underlying Stock   The Middletons don't have a lot of cash to invest ($3,000) and since option contracts usually control 100 shares of stock, they need to have enough to buy at least 100 shares if they want to trade covered calls. In their situation, without resorting to margin, they could only buy 100 shares of a $30 stock so they could sell just one contract of calls. Suppose they could get $1 a share for selling their at-the-money calls that expire in a month. They would take in $100 less a commission (usually $15 or under). Would that help? Well, $85 added to their income may not put them over the top, but it is definitely $85 better than nothing. However, suppose they could find a stock in the $10 price range where they could get 60 cents a share for selling the at-the-money calls that also expire in a month. Now, they could afford to buy 300 shares at $10 to invest their $3,000 and could now sell three contracts of the at-the-money calls for 60 cents. Instead of bringing in $100 less commission, they would now bring in $180 (300 shares × 60 cents) less commission. Assuming the same $15 (or less) commission, they now would have added $165 rather than $85 to their coffers. It is obvious that the covered call return on the $10 stock is significantly higher than on the $30 stock. The monthly return on the $30 stock before commission is 3.3 percent while the return on the $10 stock is 6.5 percent. Maybe they could find a $5 a share stock with an at-the-money option expiring in a month that has a premium of 40 cents. Now, with their $3,000, they could buy 600 shares of the stock and sell six contracts of the at-the-money calls for 40 cents thereby generating $240 or $225 after the commission. That would result in a return of 8 percent for the month.

The conclusion is that you can often obtain significantly higher returns selling at-the-money covered calls on lower priced stocks than you can on higher priced stocks. In general, when I employ a classic covered call strategy, I use stocks in the $7.50 to about the $15 range. I often can find some decent percentage returns selling calls on stocks in this price range. I tend to stay away from anything much cheaper because cheap stocks frequently are cheap for a valid reason.

One online brokerage firm I use has a search feature that permits me to input parameters such as stock price, stock volume, option expiration, open interest, and minimum return sought. When searching for covered call candidates, I normally choose price range between about $7.50 and $15 a share with an expiration from 10 to 45 days out, and a minimum unexercised return of 2 percent (for the short term before expiration). I took a little break from writing and just performed that search. I chose at-the-money calls with an expiration 41 days away since the near options expire in just 11 days, stocks priced between $7.50 and $15 that trade an average of at least 250,000 shares a day (for liquidity), with open interest in the options of at least 250 contracts (again for liquidity), a minimum premium for the call of 50 cents, and a minimum static return (without being called out) between 2 percent and 7.5 percent. In seconds, the search revealed 22 candidates that fit my criteria with returns ranging from 2.94 percent to 7.18 percent. At this point, it is important to continue the selection process rather than just choose the one with the highest return. Often the candidates with the highest returns are stocks whose price is falling so there is a real danger that the stock price will fall more than the amount I receive for the option. These candidates are often bearish and I reject them if they are not in an uptrend or at least coming off a support. It doesn't take very long to see which ones are falling, which are flat, and which are rising so from a list of 22 I might wind up with only a play or two, and that's fine.

Now I have some bullish stocks that I can buy and sell covered calls to achieve a 3 percent or 4 percent return on my investment in little more than a month.

Time Frame   In the classic strategy, when I am selling covered calls, I regularly sell only calls that have a relatively short time until expiration. Since I am selling at-the-money calls, the whole premium I am selling is for the time value. As with any option, time is the enemy of the buyer and friend of the seller. All other things being equal, as a seller of calls, I am making money as time passes and the closer to expiration, the faster the time value diminishes, which is to the detriment of the call buyer. The only way the call buyer can make money is if the stock goes up in price fairly quickly. If he only buys a short amount of time, the clock is ticking against him and the closer it gets to expiration without an upward stock price move, the less likely he will be to profit. As the seller of the option, all of that is to my advantage, particularly when we see that time value disappears faster and faster the closer it is to expiration.

Getting Assigned   Getting assigned means that the call buyer has exercised his option to buy my stock. In other words, the stock price at expiration is at or above the strike price of the call I sold. In the classic covered call strategy, I want to get called out. If the options are exercised, that means I have made the maximum I can on the play. Suppose I bought 1,000 shares of XYZ stock at $7.10 a share and immediately sold the near month $7.50 calls for 60 cents. My investment would be $7,100 and I would take in $600 or a return on investment of 8.4 percent. Not bad for a month, but what if the stock went to $7.85 by expiration? Now I would be assigned and my stock purchased for $7.50 (the strike price at which I agreed to sell) and I would take in $7,500. That means that I not only got the 60 cents for selling the call, which I get to keep no matter what, I also made another 40 cents a share or $400 on the stock sale. Now, instead of an 8.4 percent return for the month, I have made a total of $1,000 on my $7,100 initial investment or a return of 14 percent instead of 8.4 percent in the month. It is true that I no longer have the stock, but so what, I have a great profit and $8,100 to invest for the next month.

What If the Stock Price Drops?   Using the same example as in the previous paragraph, suppose that the stock price falls after I have sold the covered call. I paid $7.10 a share for the stock and the market paid me 60 cents to sell the near term $7.50 call so my net investment (ignoring commissions for the example) is $6.50, so as long as the stock stays at $6.50 or above, the worst thing that can happen is a break even or better. If the stock price hit $6.80 at expiration, I would keep the $600 I got for selling the calls and could either sell more calls for the next month or simply sell the stock. If I sold the stock, I would lose 30 cents a share on the stock, but would have gained 60 cents on the calls so with 1,000 shares, I would still have made $300 overall or a return of 4.2 percent for the month. The real issue arises if the stock price goes below my breakeven of $6.50. In that case, I have several options depending on when the price fell below the $6.50. If it is at expiration, I would probably just sell the stock and take my loss. If, for example, the stock had fallen to $6.10, I would have a 40-cent loss. However, what if the stock dropped with a couple of weeks until expiration? As the stock price falls, I am losing money on the stock, but gaining money on the call. Suppose the stock is at $6.40, it is quite likely that the premium on the $7.50 calls has fallen dramatically. Let's say those calls can now be purchased for $0.10. I could buy to close my calls for 10 cents thereby achieving a gain on the calls of 50 cents (sold for 60 cents, bought back for 10 cents) on the calls and then would sell the stock at $6.40, losing 70 cents a share on the stock. Overall, I would have only a 20-cent loss and be out of the play and on to the next. The reason I buy to close the call position first and then sell the stock is so that I will not be in a naked call position. Naked calls can be dangerous and unless you are a Level 5 trader (in which case you probably aren't reading this anyway), your broker probably won't let you do it.

A Little Variation—Selling in the Money Calls   I have emphasized the sale of at-the-money calls because they provide the highest premium in terms of time value, but, of course, the seller can choose any available strike to sell. Let's say we found a $10 stock that is performing a little erratically, but has a $1.50 at-the-money premium. We are concerned that the stock may drift lower to its next support around $8. If we sold the $10 call and brought in $1.50 but the stock price did fall to $8, we would be upside down. We bought the stock for $10, the market paid us $1.50 so our basis is $8.50, and the stock is now at $8. That scenario is not a particularly happy one. Since we do like the high premiums the options on this stock offers, we might consider selling the in-the-money $7.50 calls. We know those calls have intrinsic value of $2.50 plus some time value that will be somewhat less than the time value on the $10 calls so the $7.50 calls may be trading around $3.30 ($2.50 intrinsic value + $0.80 time value). If we sold the $7.50 calls, we bring in $3.30 a share. As long as the stock is above $7.50 at expiration, we will be called out and we'll lose $2.50 a share on the stock, but we get to keep the $3.30 we were paid for the option, so while we are losing the $2.50 on the stock, we still made 80 cents on the calls. Now we have created a situation where we still make money even if the stock price drops 25 percent. While selling in-the-money calls does not ordinarily realize a return as high as selling at-the-money calls, it does have the benefit of creating a little cushion for the stock price to fall and still return an overall profit.

Other Choices for the Middletons

We have seen how folks with relatively small amounts to invest can leverage the covered call strategy a bit by selling calls on lower priced stocks and how that strategy can result in a significant return over time. Another method to obtain leverage is also available to them as it would be to others, like Forrest Footloose who may be looking at even greater returns on small investments. We'll look at that strategy in the next section.

FORREST FOOTLOOSE USES LEAPS AS THE UNDERLYING

Forrest Footloose shares a couple of things with the Middletons. Both have little cash to invest, but both would benefit greatly from the ability to add some regular income to help pay the bills every month. Buying cheaper stocks as we saw in the preceding section on the classic covered call strategy is certainly one way to achieve that end, but it is not the only way. The markets offer many ways to create income and vary risk.

In this section, we will address the use of LEAPS as a vehicle to seek capital appreciation as well as to provide an underlying against which a trader can also regularly sell calls to provide income. When I write about an underlying, I mean something that is analogous to a stock for the purpose of writing covered calls. LEAPS is an acronym for the full technical name:

Long Term Equity Anticipation Securities. LEAPS are similar to options although they have a longer time until expiration. Ordinarily, LEAPS expire a year to three years from the time of purchase. They can be traded the same as options. I should mention that when we refer to LEAPS, it always has the "S" and there is no such investment vehicle known as a LEAP. Also, as you have probably noticed by now, all the letters are capitalized. If you talk to someone who is trading a "Leap," for example, you may want to be a little cautious about taking his advice and explore a little further before taking any of his advice about trading.

A Few Comparisons between LEAPS and Stock Ownership

If we look first at risk, whether we buy stock or we buy LEAPS calls, the initial risk is what we invest. If we buy a stock for $30 a share, our risk is what we paid for the stock. The same is true if we buy a LEAPS call. If we pay $10 a share for a contract (usually consisting of 100 shares), our risk is $10 a share. In each case, our whole investment is at risk. However, LEAPS differ from stock ownership in that they expire while stocks don't. When we buy a LEAPS call, for example, we know exactly when it will expire and that could be as far out as about three years. Since LEAPS do expire, at the time we buy LEAPS calls, they are going to be cheaper than buying the stock.

When we consider it, though, for whatever period remains before a LEAPS call will expire, we control the stock even though we don't own it. As with any call option, when we buy a LEAPS call, we have entered a contract that gives us the right, but not the obligation, to buy the stock at any time before expiration for the strike price we bought. As an example, as I write, Caterpillar, Inc. (CAT) is trading just above $70 a share. Right now, I could buy the $70 LEAPS with expiration a year and a half out for about $12 a share. If I bought 1,000 shares of the stock, my investment would be $70,000, while buying the $70 LEAPS calls, it would only be $12,000 (10 contracts × 100 shares per contract × $12 a share). Now, anytime in the next year and a half, I have the right to buy the stock for $70, even if it went to $100 or more a share. In the sense that we have a right to buy the stock for an extended period of time at a specific price, we control the shares.

A couple of things we don't get when we buy the LEAPS calls rather than the stock are dividends and the right to vote in shareholder elections. Missing out on dividends can be a drawback, but one that can be overcome as you'll see as we explore the strategy I'm about to discuss. Even though you lack the right to vote in a corporate election when you control only a miniscule proportion of the outstanding shares, it is probably of little consequence.

In exchange for expiring in the future, LEAPS calls have the distinct advantage of providing significant leverage. Just look at the CAT example and you will see that we could buy the stock at $70 a share or we could control the stock at that same $70 price for a year and a half for $12 a share. If we bought 1,000 shares of stock, our risk would be $70,000; if we bought 10 contracts of the LEAPS calls to control the same number of shares, our risk would be $12,000. As we'll soon see, this great leverage can help us achieve a much greater percentage return selling short-term calls against our LEAPS position than we could achieve selling covered calls against the stock.

For the same amount of money, we can control a whole lot more shares than we can if we bought the stock. Suppose young Forrest Footloose had some interest in investing, but only had $1,400 to work with. He could not buy enough shares of CAT at the $70 level to even sell a single contract of calls against his position. He would need $7,000 plus commission to buy 100 shares so he just doesn't have enough capital to even get started trading covered calls on CAT. On the other hand, he could buy a single contract of the $70 calls with expiration a year out. At $12 a share and with the LEAPS contract covering 100 shares, it would cost $1,200 plus a commission to buy the contract. With his $1,400, Forrest has enough to control a 100-share position in CAT. Later in this chapter, I'll show how owning LEAPS calls can result in some pretty astonishing returns, but right now our emphasis is on bringing in some income so let's look at the strategy.

Call Calendar Spreads: Selling Calls Using LEAPS Instead of Stock as the Underlying

Call calendar spreads is the fancy term for option trades that are much like trading covered calls against stock. If we break down the term call calendar spreads, it is obvious that the strategy is going to use calls, that something is spread, and it involves a calendar. From the last section, you know that one of the elements of the calendar spread will be buying a LEAPS call. That position is akin to owning the stock, only cheaper. Once we own those LEAPS calls, we can sell other options (like writing a covered call) with an expiration that isn't so far away (that's the calendar part). The spread is the distance apart in months so we could buy a LEAPS that expires in three years and sell a call that expires next month and have a calendar spread. If the strike we sell in the nearer month is the same as the strike we bought in our LEAPS position, it is a plain old calendar spread. If the strikes of the two positions are different and the expiration months are different, it is called a diagonalized calendar spread. It's that simple. What is a new vocabulary for many may be the hardest part. I think new traders can become more at ease if they first just understand what they are trying to accomplish and then understand how they are going to go about it (that is the next thing on our agenda). After understanding the concepts they can then worry about the terminology.

Using this strategy, all we are going to do is buy some LEAPS calls and use them as the underlying. We'll then sell other calls against the position to generate income. It is similar to writing covered calls against stock, but there are some important differences that we'll review as we go forward.

What LEAPS Calls to Buy   My personal preference when buying LEAPS calls is to buy in-the-money calls. When I enter the position, I look for a delta around .70 which simply means that for each dollar the stock moves up or down the option premium is expected to move approximately 70 cents. As the stock price increases, the delta normally is expected to increase as well until the call is deep in the money when the delta can approach one and the call premium essentially moves dollar for dollar with the stock price. That method can be quite profitable if the stock price is making a strong upward move. Buying in-the-money calls also ordinarily permits the trader to sell other calls against the LEAPS position relatively quickly as opposed to the situation that arises when buying at-the-money or out-of-the-money calls. One significant difference between writing calls against LEAPS calls and writing covered calls against stock we own is that while it is fine to be called out of a stock position, we want to avoid exercise of the calls we sell when our underlying is a LEAPS call. The reason to avoid exercise in the LEAPS situation is that our LEAPS calls will have both intrinsic value and time value and we do not want to lose the time value portion.

A trader certainly can buy at-the-money or out-of-the-money LEAPS calls, but they will be buying a lower delta and may have some difficulty in selling other calls against the LEAPS until the stock price has moved up.

What Calls to Sell   As a general rule, whenever I am selling options, I like to sell the shortest time available, but rarely any more than six weeks until expiration. In circumstances where the underlying is a LEAPS call position, I sell short-term out-of-the-money calls. As you may remember from the classic covered call discussion in this chapter, when we sell out-of-the-money calls, the premium consists completely of time value and the closer to expiration, the faster that time value diminishes. Since we are selling short amounts of time, we can expect the time value to run in our favor faster and faster as the option approaches expiration and, as soon as it expires, we can repeat the process by selling the next month calls to bring in even more income.

Examples can be helpful and the following discussion will use prices that are actual and current as of the time I am writing this section. Since a relatively significant amount of time will pass between the time this section is written and the time you read it, the numbers will have changed so please be aware that these are examples only and, in all probability, will present a different scenario when you are studying this material.

Example: Selling Calls against LEAPS on a Moderately Priced Stock—$12^1/_4$ Percent Return in 37 Days with a Calendar Spread

In July 2008, Qualcom (QCOM) had been trending up for most of the year and was currently around $47.60 a share. The Jan 2010 42.50 LEAPS calls were trading around $12.25 a share and had a delta of .69. A trader would buy one contract of those calls for $1,225 (1 contract × 100 shares per contract × $12.25 per share) plus commission. The 2010 calls had 555 days until expiration. Since there were only nine days to expiration of the July contract, I looked at the Aug calls and found I could sell the Aug 50 calls for about $1.50 a share less the commission. Those calls would expire in 37 days and before commission would offer a return of $12^1/_4$ percent for that period. As long as the stock price remained below $50 until Aug expiration, there would be nothing to do. The $1.50 a share ($150 on 100 shares) would be mine to keep in any event and I could re-peat the process the next month. The 50 calls were only one strike out of the money so I could have chosen the 52.50 calls that were trading around $0.80 and would present a less likely chance of being called out. Selling those would have resulted in a 37-day return of $6^1/_2$ percent. Assuming that a trader could sell two strikes out-of-the-money 10 times during the course of the next year, he could enjoy a before commission return of 65 per-cent in addition to the possible appreciation of his LEAPS calls if the stock continued trending upward.

Example: Selling Calls against LEAPS on a High Priced Stock—How to Make 9.5 Percent in about a Month versus 2 Percent in the Same Time

While this may not be something Forrest and his $1,200 could do right away, buying LEAPS calls on a very expensive stock is a way that people with smaller accounts might trade and gain fairly large dollar income each month. Google (GOOG) was trading at about $550 a share in July 2008. One hundred shares would require a $55,000 investment (half that on margin where you are borrowing money from the broker to buy the stock), but a trader could buy the Jan 2010 at-the-money $550 calls for about $110 a share. One contract would still require a fairly hefty $11,000 investment, but that is only about 20 percent of what the stock would cost. In this case, the at-the-money calls would have a delta around .61. Though I usually prefer in-the-money calls, I see here that I could sell the Aug 600 calls, again with a little over a month until expiration for about $10.50 to bring in $1,050 or a return for five weeks of

9.5 percent before commission. Compare that to stock ownership where 100 shares would cost $55,000 and the 600 calls would still generate $1,050 or a return of only about 2 percent.

What to Do If the Stock Price Goes Up   As far as the LEAPS calls are concerned, it is a good thing when the stock price goes up because we can expect the value of those calls to go up as well. If we own LEAPS calls with a delta of .70, for example, and the stock price increases by $5 a share, our calls should move up by about $3.50 a share. The problem arises when the stock price goes higher than the strike price of the calls we sold. As I mentioned earlier, when we are selling calls with the LEAPS calls as our underlying, we do not want to be called out because we could lose the time value in our LEAPS. Suppose from Example 1 in the preceding section that we bought the $42.50 strike LEAPS calls on QCOM for $12.25 a share when the stock was trading at $47.60 a share. When we entered the position our calls had a delta of .69 upon entry. We then decided to sell the 50 Aug calls (five weeks to expiration) for $1.50 a share. Since the calls we sold had little time before expiration and were out of the money, they would have a lower delta, in this case around .35. While we were in those positions, suppose several days passed and the stock suddenly ran up to $52. Now, the calls we sold are $2 in the money and we run the risk of an assignment. Remember, when we are selling calls against LEAPS calls, we want to avoid being called out. What can we do? One approach is to close the Aug 50 position by buying to close those calls. Initially, we "sold to open" the Aug 50s for $1.50, now we would "buy to close" that Aug 50 leg. Since the stock price is now $52, we know that the $50 calls are $2 in the money so we are going to have to pay at least $2 intrinsic value plus some time value to close the position. If the time value is now $0.80, we are going to have to pay $2.80 a share to close a position that we opened for only $1.50 so we are going to suffer a $1.30 a share loss on that leg. However, remember that the delta on our LEAPS calls started at .69 while the delta on the leg we sold was only .35. For every $1 the stock price increased, initially, the Aug calls increased by 35 cents. However, for every $1 the stock price increased, initially, our LEAPS calls increased by 69 cents. As the stock price increased, so, too, would the delta, but the point is that the delta on the LEAPS will always be greater than the delta on the short-term calls we sold. We can expect, therefore, that the gain on the LEAPS call premium will be greater than the loss we will take by closing the Aug position. Now, we can also sell another higher strike price for Aug or the next expiration.

What to Do If the Stock Price Falls   Writing covered calls is a bullish strategy. Whether we buy stock and sell covered calls or we buy LEAPS calls and sell other calls we want the stock price to go up, or at the worst, stay even. What if the stock price falls? There are a number of alternatives. We can just close any calls we have sold and then sell our LEAPS calls to exit the play completely. In that situation, we will probably make some profit on the calls we are buying back and we will probably take a somewhat larger loss on the sale of our LEAPS for an overall net loss. At least we are out from under a losing position and we can go look for another opportunity.

Another alternative if the trader wants to remain in the long LEAPS position is to roll down or roll out and down the short position. In case it isn't clear, when I write about a short position, I am referring to the position I sold. In order to roll down, the trader would buy to close the leg he originally sold and would sell a lower strike. In our QCOM example, we had bought the 2010 42.50 LEAPS calls and sold the Aug 50 calls for $1.50. Suppose QCOM shares fell to $40. Naturally, the price of the Aug 50 calls would drop as would the value of our LEAPS calls. If we wanted to hold the LEAPS, we could roll down by buying to close the Aug 50 calls for less than we sold them originally and generate a profit on that transaction, and, at the same time, roll down and perhaps sell the Aug 45 calls to bring in additional income. Alternatively, we could roll down to the Aug 45 calls and out to the Sept expiration by buying to close the Aug 50 calls and capturing that profit and then selling the Sept 45 calls. Since the Sept calls have an additional month until expiration, we would expect that we could sell those calls at a higher price because of the value of the extra time.

LEAPS on Splitting Stocks: Added Income

Our emphasis has been upon using LEAPS as an underlying against which we can earn income by selling calls from month to month. While that is going on, the trader should also be aware of the phenomenal power of leverage that LEAPS calls might afford in a situation where a stock splits. At times, companies might decide to split their stock. The decision might be made because the stock has reached a high price and the company's directors would like to make it more affordable and therefore more easily acquired by a wider spectrum of investors. Splits most often are 2:1, meaning that the shareholder gets two shares for every share he owned before the split and the price of the stock is halved. Immediately after the split, the investor would have twice as many shares at half the price so his investment would be the same. As an example, suppose XYZ was trading at $60 a share and the company announced a 2:1 split. An investor who owned 1,000 shares would have an asset worth $60,000 before the split. After the split, he would have 2,000 shares, but they would only be worth $30 a share so his asset would still be worth $60,000. However, since he now has twice the number of shares he could sell twice the number of covered calls. If he had been selling 10 contracts of at-the-money calls each month for $1 he would have been getting $1,000 a month income. After the split, however, he would be able to sell 20 contracts instead of 10 so he might be able to generate $2,000 a month selling at-the-money calls.

Potential for Incredible Appreciation

That's really good, but it can get even better. Often following a split the share price goes higher and at times returns to the area of the presplit price. If that should occur, and in our example the price gets back up to the $60 range, the investor will have doubled his money. That is really good, but it can get even better. What happens when you own an option and there is a stock split? In the case of a 2:1 split, the number of calls you own doubles and the strike price halves. So, if we have 10 contracts of the 60 calls before the split, we will have 20 contracts of the 30 calls following the split.

Take a look at how powerful this strategy can be in the case of a split. Purely hypothetically, though the starting numbers are taken from the actual prices of a stock with a split history at the time of this writing, suppose XYZ is trading at $68.50 a share and we buy 10 contracts of the $65 LEAPS calls for $12.75. We have invested $12,750. We have been selling two strike out-of-the money calls for a few months and bringing in about $1 a share or $1,000 each month and then XYZ announces a 2:1 split. We now have 20 contracts of the 32.50 calls and our cost per share is reduced to $6.38 a share. Now, the stock price starts to climb again and over the next six months gets back up to the $65 range. How are we doing? Well, we have been selling 20 instead of 10 contracts of the two strike out-of-the money calls so if we got 75 cents a share average, we would be bringing in $1,500 a month. But look at the value of our calls now. We have the right to buy 2,000 shares of XYZ at $32.50 and the stock is trading at $65. We could buy the stock for $65,000 ($32.50 a share × 2,000 shares) and simultaneously sell it for $130,000 ($65 a share × 2,000). That is a $65,000 profit on our initial investment of $12,750 plus what we made selling the calls. The profit on the calls alone, without even considering the $1,000 or $2,000 a month we made while waiting for this to happen, is equal to a return of almost 510 percent!

Let's stretch our imagination and suppose we had bought those same 10 calls and there was a second 2:1 split. From 20 contracts with a $32.50 strike we would now have 40 contracts with a strike of $16.25. Then let's say the stock moved up to $46.25 a share (to make the math easy). Now we could buy 4,000 shares at $16.25 and immediately sell them for $46.25. That would be a $30 gain per share on 4,000 shares or a $120,000 profit before the commission or a return of better than 940 percent without even including the monthly income we brought in from selling calls against our position.

These are incredibly powerful numbers. But, you say, that just couldn't happen. No stock is going to split that often. Take a look at Microsoft (MSFT), which split three times in three years, or Dell Computer (DELL), which split five times in $2^1/_4$ years, or Krispy Kreme Doughnuts (KKD), which split twice in three months, or Taser International (TASR), which had a 3:1 split in February 2004 and then a 2:1 split just two months later and another 2:1 split seven months after that.

Please don't get the wrong idea. These situations are by no means common. Nevertheless, on occasion they present extraordinary opportunities for traders and potentially mind-boggling returns as an adjunct to a simple income-producing strategy.

 GETTING INTO GEAR

In this chapter we examined some ways to generate income, and we have seen how a buy-and-hold investor might consider using covered calls to enhance overall portfolio performance, or how someone with some interest in trading might add a stream of income employing a classic covered call strategy, or how LEAPS calls might be used as one leg of a call calendar spread to generate regular reasonably high monthly percentage returns. Finally, we touched upon the potential power provided by LEAPS ownership in relatively rare split situations.

In Chapter 5, we'll look at investments that provide a decent dividend yield to create added income while also offering the chance to capture trading gains beyond the income flow.

Trading for Investors with No Time to Trade

Equities with High Yields

We really don't need anyone to tell us that we are busy. According to a Bureau of Labor Statistics News Release back on June 25, 2007, the average American worker was doing about 20 percent of his work at home. Not only are we working at home more, we are also adding to the number of jobs we have and are encouraged to become even more productive. Lack of time is one of the most common reasons why many people avoid trading. In spite of all the modern time-saving devices like the computer, Internet shopping, robotic vacuum cleaners, microwaves, it seems like we have less and less time. Folks like our hypothetical Middleton family are involved in an ever-escalating rat race in which greater and greater productivity is demanded just to stay even, where they have been swamped with debt and have resorted to two or three jobs to try to keep up with their own spending, and where their devotion to children has led them to enroll the kids in and drive them to every organized activity known to man. After all those things, there are Home Owners Association meetings, charitable events, community gatherings, shopping, doctors' visits, vehicle maintenance, religious activities, and political activities to name but a few of the many bites taken from their clocks and calendars before they even think of leisure time or their own investments.

A natural response to these demands is, "No wonder I can't get ahead; there aren't enough hours in the day!" It is tough to have time for everything, so investing is often put near the bottom of the list. But doesn't it seem that we might have more time if we had more money? Added income from other sources could reduce or eliminate the necessity to work that third job and maybe enable us to quit the second job as well. Wouldn't it be great to free up time like that? If Tim Middleton or anyone in his boat would make investing a high priority, he might be able to accomplish the objectives of freeing up time and enhancing quality of life.

Even if we do elevate investing on our list of priorities, the time we have to devote to investments is likely to be extremely limited. Or, the fact may be that we just don't want to devote much time to our investments. I may prefer to select some high-yielding investments and go bone fishing in the Florida Keys, or cast a fly to some silver salmon in Alaska, or hit some golf balls. It doesn't matter what else a trader might want to do, there is no reason why he shouldn't still be bringing in income even while he is relaxing in the sun on Kauai. With little effort, almost anyone can identify some investments that provide a relatively lucrative return and that require only minimal monitoring.

Certain categories of investments are specifically designed to operate as income producers. As we'll see in the remainder of this chapter, some of these investments also incorporate the ability to achieve additional income through the sale of covered calls as well as having the potential to create significant capital gains through trading just like any stock. In other words, many of the vehicles in these categories can work well even with little attention from the investor. In these investments, with only a little added effort, the investor can achieve results that are magnified well beyond an already good base return.

As I write this book, many of the specific investments in this chapter are yielding 8 percent to 12 percent a year without any effort beyond entering the investment. Some are even federally tax-free investments yielding 6 percent or more and paying their dividends each month. To put a 12 percent return in perspective, we might look to the Rule of 72. The Rule of 72 provides a rough calculation of how long it takes a sum to double when interest is compounded at a specific rate. To determine roughly how long it will take an investment to double, we divide 72 by the annual percentage so if we were receiving 10 percent compound interest, it would take about 7.2 years for our sum to double ($72 \div 10 = 7.2$). Of course, that calculation does not account for taxes. To see the power, suppose we had $10,000 in a Roth IRA and found an investment yielding 12 percent a year. Our investment would double approximately every six years ($72 \div 12 = 6$). In six years we would have $20,000, in 12 years $40,000, in 18 years $80,000, and in 24 years $160,000. Those results don't seem too shabby when we consider that our only effort was to find and make the investment in the first place. Imagine what could be accomplished with a little extra effort. Where could this investment wind up just adding 1 percent to 3 percent selling covered calls each month?

The categories we'll examine in this chapter will include Master Limited Partnerships (MLPs) that we touched on in Chapter 3, Real Estate

Investment Trusts (REITs), and closed-end funds. Each of these categories includes investments that produce high returns and often offer some additional specific advantages to the investor.

MASTER LIMITED PARTNERSHIPS (MLPs)

We took a quick look at Master Limited Partnerships (MLPs) in Chapter 3. By way of review, these investments are in partnerships rather than in corporations. When we buy a stock, we are buying ownership in a corporation. When we invest in an MLP, we are entering into a partnership. We become limited partners and our risk is limited to the amount we invest. One of the critical differences between the two entities, corporation and limited partnership, is the way income is treated. Corporations pay income tax on their net income after allowable deductions; the partnership entity does not pay income taxes itself, but, instead, the tax liability is passed on to the partners or unit holders. In the case of an MLP, the partners receive a K-1 form each year detailing their shares of net income. The partners then pay income tax on the net amount at their own individual rates based upon the income reflected in the K-1.

The cash distributions made to the limited partners are different from what we normally think of dividends in that the MLP distributions are *not* taxed when they are received, but, instead, are treated as reductions in the cost basis of the units or shares. Corporate dividends are subject to the payment of income tax when they have been received. Since the MLP distributions serve to reduce the cost basis in the investment, the tax is effectively deferred until the investment is actually sold.

By law, MLPs must earn a high percentage of their income through natural resources, real estate, or commodities in order to qualify for the tax benefits, but once qualified, not only have the advantage of no income tax at the partnership level, but also have some other important tax advantages including the ability to depreciate assets. Probably most commonly, MLPs are in business related to oil and natural gas extraction or transportation. The result for the investor is often that he will receive more in cash distributions than the amount on which he will be taxed. Naturally, once the investor sells his investment, he is responsible for paying taxes on his capital gains.

While the tax advantages enumerated above are effective as of the time of this writing, I would encourage the reader not to assume they are the same at the time he reads this section. The current rules are quite favorable to investors, but, depending on politics, may change in the future. While I believe MLPs can be a very attractive investment, the prudent investor should definitely consult a tax professional before investing in them to be certain that the rules are still advantageous at the time he considers investing.

These partnerships have another plus in that they trade just like stocks and, therefore, are reasonably liquid and trade regularly on the open market. It seems like the general investing public has not yet become aware of the benefits and potential of MLPs as investments so the investor should be aware that volume is a little light as of now. In looking at a representative group as I write, it appears that daily volume runs from a low of about 30,000 or 40,000 shares per day on the lesser traded to more than half a million shares per day on the more actively traded MLPs. I note this as a caution to those who might consider taking large positions. It may well be easier to exit a position in the more actively traded issues in the event there is a need or desire to close a position quickly.

As I suggested in Chapter 3, a review of about 20 MLPs that I keep on a personal watch list revealed distributions in the 5 percent to 9 percent per year range, and many are also optionable so that the investor who wants to do just a little more work may be able to pump up his returns by selling covered calls against his position. Optionability also enables an investor to buy protective puts to reduce overall risk in the investment if he chooses. For people who may not be familiar with protective puts, it may be helpful to understand that you can buy a "put," which is an option contract that gives the buyer the right (but not the obligation) to force someone to buy his shares at a specified price within a predetermined time. In order to obtain that right, the person who buys a put pays the seller a premium much like one would pay an insurance company a premium to protect against loss.

Finally, as with the other two categories we'll examine in this chapter (REITs and closed-end funds), MLPs can be actively traded so that the investor can buy on upturns following dips and sell on downturns following highs. In this manner, the more active trader may be able to add to income from distributions and sales of covered calls to generate even higher returns.

Appendix B lists several MLPs that I regularly watch that have options as well as the distributions discussed earlier.

REAL ESTATE INVESTMENT TRUSTS (REITs)

Over the course of time, investments in real estate have produced great profits and made many millionaires. Though real estate hit a downdraft in the mid- to late 2000s as a result of the subprime mortgage debacle, it is still in limited supply and at some point will likely climb in value once again. As with stock, buy low and sell high (along with location, location, location) is the real estate investors' mantra. Many investors don't even consider real estate because they are concerned that it will require too large an investment, or that management may be a hassle they do not want to take on, or that the carrying costs would be prohibitive.

Not long ago, a small down payment and some creative financing could provide great leverage in a real estate investment. However, lending practices have changed recently because of the inability and sometimes unwillingness of borrowers to meet their obligations and the resulting pressure on financial institutions sometimes leading to failure. The financial institutions are now playing defense and trying to protect themselves from further losses such as those occasioned by their earlier failures in overlending to borrowers whose inability to pay should have been evident in the first place. Just as individual traders can cause themselves great pain when greed motivates their trading, so, too, can some financial institutions get themselves into trouble when their greed for more and more loans outweighs the prudent decision to refuse high-risk or subprime loans. In any event, there are a variety of reasons why an investor may not want to buy or may not be able to buy real estate even though he recognizes the high profit potential that may be available.

For investors who see wisdom in real estate, but who may not have the time or resources to devote to owning property, there is good news in the form of the Real Estate Investment Trust or REIT. REITs are corporations that invest in real estate and meet certain criteria so that somewhat like MLPs in the energy area, they are able to significantly reduce or eliminate income taxes at the corporate level. In order to achieve that status, REITs must meet a number of criteria, including requirements that they must be managed by trustees or a board of directors and must have the legal form of a corporation, association, or trust, and must have transferable shares. That latter requirement translates into the ability to trade REITs on the open market just like a stock. They are also required to hold at least 75 percent of their investment assets in real estate and at least 75 percent of their income must come from rents or mortgage interest. An additional requirement, and important benefit to shareholders, is that a REIT must pay dividends equal to at least 90 percent of their taxable income. In many cases, that requirement to pay 90 percent of taxable income results in a relatively high return for shareholders.

Currently, there are roughly 200 REITs available to investors. The price per share or unit runs the gamut from under $5 to well over $100 so there is a price range available to everyone. At the time of this writing, the dividends I researched ran from around 3.5 percent per year to more than 20 percent. Though some REITs have seen added volatility recently resulting from some of the credit issues mentioned earlier, in general, the investments have not experienced great volatility over extended periods of time. Also, as one might expect, the long-term trend has been up overall, even considering the credit crisis. Naturally, some categories of real estate have performed better than others in the recent past. As I write this chapter, industrial REITs, for example, have hardly skipped a beat in their climb while retail REITs, as a class, fell over 30 percent from a high in early 2007 until the middle of 2008.

In addition to the requirement that they pay out 90 percent of their taxable income in order to maintain their tax benefits, many REITs have the advantage of specializing in certain segments of the market so the investor can tailor his investments to favor one sector or another depending on current conditions. REITs are available, for instance, in the industrial, retail, healthcare facilities, hotel/motel, office, and residential sectors so the investor can maintain holdings in real estate while trading out of one segment on downturns and entering a different segment that is moving forward. For people unwilling or unable to trade in and out of positions to maximize gains, there are even REIT Exchange-Traded Funds (ETFs) that manage a broader spectrum of REITs under a single investment. An example of such an ETF (and I'll be talking a lot more about ETFs in the next section) is the Vanguard REIT ETF (VNQ).

As I grew more successful in my own trading, I invested in some resort real estate in Kauai and in Arizona. I am very happy with those investments, but care and management of the properties is time-consuming and things like HOA (homeowners' association) fees, taxes, insurance, and maintenance fees can become expensive. In addition, though I have competent management companies, there is always concern for the treatment and condition of the properties as an absentee owner. Since we use these properties ourselves at different times of the year, the investments work well overall for our purposes, but obviously, this type of investment in real estate is not for everyone. As a pure investment, REITs enable the investor to include real estate in his portfolio, but the headaches of property management, taxes, and insurance are of no immediate concern.

A couple of years ago, while cruising Alaska in a small 10 cabin boat, I had the pleasure of meeting the CEO of a prominent retail REIT engaged in shopping centers. Not only was I impressed by him, I also was impressed by the work done on behalf of his investors. Having practiced law for many years, I was aware of the many hoops through which a developer must jump in order to create a large shopping center from scratch. Everything from building new roads to dealing with municipal bureaucracies to design to pleasing the plumbing inspector to finding responsible tenants is included in the mix. The REIT management is taking care of those time-consuming, burdensome, tear-your-hair-out tasks while the investor enjoys a stream of regular income from his investment along with the potential for capital appreciation.

As we also saw with MLPs, many REITs also offer options so the investor with the inclination can trade covered calls against his position as well as collecting the dividend income. Whenever options are available, the investor also has the ability to insure his position by buying protective puts.

In Appendix C, I have compiled a list of REITs with options in various sectors as a starting point for the investor who may want to make an income-producing investment in real estate. While the companies I have included in Appendix C were trading reasonable daily volume at the time I prepared the Appendix, it is always prudent to check recent volumes to make sure there is sufficient liquidity to make sure you can get out of a position fairly rapidly if you decide to exit. As a general rule of thumb with REITs, I would look for an average daily volume of at least 250,000 shares and, if less than that, I do not want to hold a position where the number of shares I own is more than 10 percent of the average daily volume.

FIRST, A WORD ABOUT OPEN-END FUNDS

Most of us are familiar with mutual funds. They are the investment vehicles sold to the public by investment companies. The funds obtained from investors are then used to buy investments and pay administrative and management fees. What we commonly think of as mutual funds are open-end funds. The number of shares fluctuates from day to day and depends on money flowing in from new investors or investors adding to already existing positions or from money flowing out to investors who are redeeming their shares. The funds can grow quite large since investors can continue to invest money as long as the fund permits.

Since open-end funds are subject to redemption at any time, the funds must keep cash on hand in order to pay the investor for the shares he is redeeming. Commonly, the share value for redemption is the NAV (net asset value) at the end of the day so an investor could place an order to sell his position in the morning when the market is soaring, and wind up receiving much less if the fund's investments took a big downturn as the trading day unfolded. Often, these open-end mutual funds require a minimum investment and, invariably, charge management fees.

The management fees for open-end funds should be a serious consideration for investors since the effect of those fees on value means that the investments made by the fund managers must exceed their percentage before the investor can achieve a profit. As I mentioned earlier, cash must be kept on hand to redeem shares and that cash is not available to invest. In order to profit overall, after fees, the return on the amount actually invested has to generate a higher percentage return just to achieve the same dollar return if the cash actually could have been invested. If the fund's investments wind up the year flat, the investor loses a percentage of his money because the fund makes the charges whether it makes money or not. It may be worth it if the manager has done a good job and made a decent profit (greater than the S&P, for example), but I have always wondered why I should pay someone to lose my money. I could do that myself. If the fund can't do better than the S&P, why pay someone good money to do what you can do yourself just by buying an Exchange-Traded Fund (ETF) that tracks the index?

As you probably have guessed, I am not a huge fan of open-end funds. One of the reasons for my tepid view of open-end funds is that I believe there are a number of better vehicles for an investor. One of those vehicles is the ETF that I'll address in greater detail toward the end of this chapter, and another we'll examine here is the closed-end fund.

A BETTER CHOICE: CLOSED-END FUNDS

Unlike the open-end fund, closed-end funds have a fixed number of shares and can be traded just like a stock. If an investor perceives something is not going well, he can close his position at any time. He does not have to wait until the end of day NAV has been calculated. He can also enter a position on an upturn from a dip if he chooses. In short, he has more control over his entry and exit strategy. Since the closed-end fund has a fixed number of shares, there is no requirement that cash be kept on hand so the whole fund can be invested. Shares simply trade and there is no redemption as with the open-end fund. Share value is determined by the market and can be above or below the actual NAV. As I was writing this section, I checked and found several of the closed-end funds that were actually trading below their NAV value. (Nuveen Investments has a handy web site that actually shows a comparison between the actual share price and the NAV. You can find it at www.etfconnect.com.)

Closed-end funds also have managers who are well paid so the investor should be aware of those fees as well. However, nonperformance is generally reflected in share price decline and can be the signal for an investor to put his money elsewhere whether it is in another closed-end fund or some other investment.

I particularly like the ability to trade these closed-end funds since it allows me to place orders with my broker that can put things on autopilot and require very little monitoring, if any, on my part. The only time I need to turn my attention to these investments is at my entry and after I have received notification that my exit order has been filled. Some plans may dictate a little more hands-on time, but an investment in an open-end fund can certainly be set up, entered, and exited through orders placed before the position is even entered.

The "Autopilot Order"

I prefer trades where I have nothing more to do after I enter. It frees my time for other things since I don't have to do anything else once I have made my entry decision and decided my exit strategy. For people who may not be familiar with setting up a trade so that every element from entry to exit is in place before the trade is entered, let me walk you through an example.

Suppose I have looked at a federally tax-free closed-end municipal bond fund (XYZ) paying 6 percent per year and see that it is turning up from a dip. It is trading at $11.65 a share and I would be willing to pay up to $11.75 a share for the 1,000 shares I would like to buy. If my order to buy is filled, I am willing to let it move down as much as 5 percent from my purchase price, but if it does fall that much, I want to cut my loss at that level. At the same time, if the price moves up, I want to try to let my profits run. I want to do all this before I enter the trade and don't want to have to look at it again. The online broker I use permits many helpful orders and that is one of the reasons I use that firm. In order to accomplish my entry and exit requirements, I would place the following orders simultaneously: buy to open 1,000 shares of XYZ at a limit of $11.75 and an OTO (one triggers other) to sell XYZ on a trailing stop at 5 percent below the price, good until canceled. Now I am set. My initial order to buy assures I will not pay more than $11.75 a share. If that entry order is filled, it automatically triggers the next order to sell XYZ on a 5 percent trailing stop. The trailing stop moves with the price of the shares. If I were filled on the buy part of my order at $11.75, the stop would take me out if the price dropped 5 percent from that price (to $11.16). However, if the share price moved up, the 5 percent stop would be trailing behind it so, if, for example, the price got to $14 a share, the stop would then take me out on a 5 percent drop from that new high (or at $13.30). The 5 percent is always calculated from the high so as the price goes higher, the stop moves up automatically. Since the order is good until canceled, I am done with the trade insofar as my time is required. (I should note that some brokers define good until canceled as a specific time so check with your broker to see how long a good until canceled order will last.) Dividends will flow automatically into my account as long as I own the shares, and the trailing stop will take me out of the position whenever it drops 5 percent from whatever high it has achieved since I entered the position.

These orders are available to all stock trading, including trades of categories like ETFs, MLPs, and REITs as well as to the closed-end funds like the one set out in the example.

Regular Income

A number of closed-end funds are designed to provide a regular stream of income. Quite a few funds make monthly distributions while others pay quarterly. As I mentioned in the example in the preceding section, some funds are designed to provide income free of federal tax, and some are even double tax-free. By double tax-free, I mean that some of the closed-end funds are designed so that residents of certain states (generally the more populated states) may not have to pay either federal or state tax on the distributions. I should note that the tax benefits apply to the distributions received while the fund is owned and that taxes do have to be paid on any capital gains when the position is closed.

In addition to the tax-free funds, an investor also can find taxable funds that are invested in corporate bonds or other debt that generally provide a higher, but taxable, yield. Each investor should investigate whether the tax-free or taxable funds might work better in his own tax setting. As I write, the federally tax-free municipal bond funds I checked were yielding between about 4.5 percent and nearly 7 percent. The share prices ranged from a little more than $4 to around $15 and I found none that were optionable. I should note that some of these funds are insured and when that is the case, the investor can expect a little trade-off since the yield will generally be a little less in exchange for the relative security of insurance.

The taxable funds invest in things like corporate bonds, debt securities, loans, or preferred stocks. Since these investments ordinarily carry a higher risk than municipal bonds and since the distributions are taxable, the yields are normally going to be higher than they would be for the closed-end municipal bond funds. A quick check as I was writing this section showed yields in the 11 percent to 13 percent range.

As I discussed in Chapter 4 when we looked at using Exchange Traded Funds (ETFs) as an investment against which we could write covered calls, these closed-end funds hold a basket of investments so the failure of one does not necessarily wipe out the value of the fund and, for that reason, the funds may be preferred to an investment in a single specific bond or other debt. The risk is spread among a number of holdings rather than being dependent on one lone obligation.

Using these closed-end funds coupled with orders such as those set out in the earlier example enable an investor to create an income stream while requiring almost no effort after setting up the position. At the very worst, risk is limited to the investment less distributions, but for practical purposes, the trailing stop will normally limit actual risk to the percentage or relatively close to the percentage chosen by the investor.

GETTING INTO GEAR

In this chapter, we looked at three investment vehicles, Master Limited Partnerships (MLPs), Real Estate Investment Trusts (REITs), and closed-end funds that offer investors added income streams without the need to spend excessive time monitoring the positions. Each of these investment categories provide at least one stream of income from their distributions, and in the case of some REITs and MLPs, provide the opportunity to add a second stream of income by selling covered calls.

In the case of REITs and MLPs, distributions of otherwise taxable income are required in order for them to retain their status and the accompanying tax benefits. In the case of MLPs, the investor has the advantage of receiving tax-deferred distribution since the distributions are treated as reduction in basis rather than as interest or as income until the position is ultimately closed. While the MLP is held, the investor also enjoys his proportionate share of depreciation as reported on his K-1 form.

Closed-end funds offer certain advantages over the open-end funds that we commonly think of as mutual funds. Their tradeability enables an investor to set up an autopilot situation where the investor can choose tax-free or taxable returns, place his initial orders, and forget about it. This combination of orders is also available to stock trades, ETFs, MLPs, and REITs as well as to the closed-end funds.

In my own trading, I often hold positions in these categories. They offer reasonable returns in exchange for little effort on the investor's part and enable the investor to preplan and execute a complete trade at the time of entry. In most cases, the share prices range from low- to mid-priced so almost any investor is capable of adding at least small positions to his portfolio at any time. Since they all can be traded like stock, as long as there is liquidity, there is no problem entering or exiting a position. I like to buy on upturns from dips and sell when they break down through a trend or moving average. When one position is closed, I can look for another in one of these categories that is turning up and keep my money invested while enjoying the income flow.

CHAPTER 6

Monitoring Trades

The Possibility of Great Returns

I n the previous chapter, we looked at some investments that provided a new stream of income and have some pretty decent returns with very little time required of the investor. People like the hypothetical Middleton family might find those investments to their liking. In fact, anyone who wants more income but who can't or doesn't want to spend much time with their investments might be smart to investigate the MLPs, closed-end funds, or REITs. In this chapter, we are going to look at some ways to generate very significant income if the investor is able and willing to spend a little more time and effort. Someone like Ed Balding, whom we introduced earlier, may be interested in doing a little trading and is willing to spend an hour or so a day may be the kind of person this chapter would interest.

When we discussed the MLPs, REITs, and closed-end funds, we were looking at investments that had the potential to yield returns from 4.5 percent tax-free to a bit more than a taxable 20 percent a year. With a little additional work, the investor could also sell covered calls against his positions and add perhaps another 2 percent a month on his investment selling covered calls. In this chapter, we'll be looking at some trades that offer potential returns on risk in the 20 percent to 35 percent range—but those returns are per month, not per year. All of the trades we will discuss have limited risk that is known precisely before we ever enter the trade. In general, the maximum length of time an investor would expect to be in these positions is no longer than two to six weeks. The strategies we will discuss can be employed in up, down, or sideways markets, and can be used on any vehicle that has options including stock, ETFs, closed-end funds, or REITs. In general, gains and losses will be short-term and, as such, can be expected to be treated as ordinary income or losses for tax purposes.

The trades we are about to examine do require some monitoring and a willingness to react. Again, as with everything we have discussed so far, the trader can plan the complete trade before ever entering the positions and only needs to act if some predetermined criterion has been met.

The trades we will explore throughout the chapter will use options and will result in a credit to the investor's account the day after the trade is opened. Unlike stock trades that settle in three days, option trades settle the following day so if we open a credit option trade today, the new money will be in our account tomorrow. In effect, the market is paying us money to enter the trade. Our job will be to keep the money, or at least some of it.

THE CONCEPT OF SELLING TIME

As we move forward in this chapter, you will see that we are going to open our positions by selling someone time value. Option premiums consist of intrinsic value and time value as set out in Appendix A (Options Trading). If an option is at the money or out of the money, the premium is all for time value since there is no intrinsic value. For example, if XYZ stock is trading at $40 a share and the near month expiration $40 call is trading at $1, the person who buys the call is paying for nothing but time and hoping that the stock price increases fairly quickly, certainly before his option expires. If he were to hold until expiration, the stock price would have to be greater than $41 (ignoring commissions) for him to profit. He has the right to buy the stock for $40, but it cost him $1 option premium to buy some time for it to go higher. On the other hand, the person who sells the call has sold nothing but time and takes on the obligation to sell the stock for $40 a share at any time before expiration. He has assured himself of $1 a share coming in and since he sold the at-the-money strike price the premium he is paid is for nothing but time value. As we are all too aware, time passes quickly, and as time passes, time value diminishes (all other things being equal) at an ever-increasing rate.

We can see a similar example with selling puts. Suppose XYZ is still selling at $40 a share and we buy the near month $37.50 put for $0.30. In this case, we are buying an out-of-the-money option. We would not exercise our put to force someone to buy our stock at $37.50 if we could get $40 for the same stock on the open market, so, once again, whether we buy the put as protection or as a directional play, we are paying for nothing but time. The seller is receiving payment for that time, and unless the stock drops below $37.50 we would not exercise the put and the seller would just keep the premium. The seller is taking a risk that he might have to buy the stock at $37.50 (less the premium he got for selling the put), but the stock price would have to drop fairly rapidly by the time the option expires. If it doesn't drop fairly quickly, the time is passing and the time value is diminishing ever more rapidly so the put seller is profiting by the simple passage of time.

The whole idea with selling a diminishing asset (time) is that by selling it we can profit just by the passage of time, alone. For that reason, I really like selling options or creating spreads where the net result is a credit on entry. My observation of coaching students and unsuccessful traders is that one of the fastest ways to the poorhouse is to buy short-term at- or out-of-the-money options. It seems they fail to realize that what they are doing is betting on a very fast directional move. If they buy a short-term out-of-the-money call, the stock must move up and it must move up relatively quickly for them to make a profit. If the stock price stays the same or goes down they will lose. Each day that time passes without an upward move in the stock price, the time value is likely to fall and with it the value of their call. It is just the opposite for the seller who can expect to accrue gains as the value of what he sold drops. Now, he can buy it back for less than what he paid. In this instance, purely as a result of the passage of time, the seller profits by selling high and buying low. Notice how that is the same thing as buying low and selling high, only the option seller in these examples does it in reverse order.

PRACTICAL APPLICATION: SPREADS

As we read in the preceding examples, there are some good reasons to be an option seller rather than a buyer at least in certain circumstances. In Chapter 7, we'll look at naked option sales, but many investors may be prohibited from selling naked options by their brokers or, even if permitted, may not want to take on the risks attendant to those trades. Fortunately, there is an alternative for investors in those categories in the form of the credit spread. In creating the spread, we can achieve the goal of setting up trades where we get a credit at entry and have known limited risk. Since we would receive a credit (money coming into our account) at the time we open the trade, it would be a net sale, and, as I illustrated in the last section, I like to enter these positions with a relatively short time to expiration by selling time value only. Time is then on my side as its value drops with each passing day.

Spreads are trades that involve more than one leg. In this section, we will be talking about something called vertical credit spreads. These are spreads that involve two legs. We will be buying one leg and selling one leg, usually at the same time. The leg we sell will be nearer the money, and, therefore, will generate a higher premium than the leg we buy, which will be further out of the money. I think of the short leg (the leg we sell to open) as the cash leg and the long leg (the one we buy) as the protective leg. The short leg brings in the money and the long leg limits the potential loss in the trade assuming the stock price turns against me and I make no adjustment.

In the case of a bearish call spread, for example, we may sell the calls that are just out of the money and buy the next higher strike. Both the call we sell and the call we buy will expire at the same time. Since the call with the lower strike will command a higher premium than the call with the higher strike, we will be entering the spread with a credit coming into our account. As an example, as I am writing this section, Copart, Inc. (CPRT) is trading at about $43.50 and has just turned down over the past three days. The nearest term options for August expire in just 19 days. Since the stock looks like it might move down from here, I checked and found that I could sell the Aug 45 calls for about 80 cents a share and I could buy the Aug 50 calls for about 10 cents a share. If I set up this spread using 10 contracts a side (selling to open 10 Aug 45 calls and buying to open 10 Aug 50 calls), I would bring in $800 (10 contracts × 100 shares per contract × $0.80) for selling the 45 calls and I would pay out $100 (10 contracts × 100 shares per contract × $0.10) for buying the 50 calls. Ignoring commissions for this discussion, I would have a net credit of $700. The Aug 45 calls I sold would obligate me to sell 1,000 shares of CPRT at $45 a share if they were exercised (also called assigned). I don't own any actual shares of CPRT, so if the stock price went up and I was called out of the Aug 45s, I would have to go buy the stock to fulfill my obligation. What if the stock was trading at $56 by then? Well, if I didn't have the long position in the $50 calls, I would have to go to the open market and buy shares at $56 in order to satisfy my obligation to sell at $45. In that event, I would lose $11 a share or $11,000. Fortunately, with my spread, that would not be the case. I could exercise my long 50 call position and buy the shares at $50 instead of $56 so my loss would be $5 a share or $5,000 instead of $11,000. But, wait: remember that the market actually paid me $700 just to enter the trade. I get to keep that $700 so the worst it could be would be a $4,300 loss, not a $5,000 loss.

Is the whole thing worth the risk? Before you answer that question for yourself, ask yourself what you consider to be a good return on investments a year or a month or whatever. The answer students usually give at the beginning of our classes is 10 percent to 15 percent a year. What is your answer for you?

In our example trade, the potential return on risk is 16.3 percent—but that is for 19 days, not for a year! The credit we got at entry ($700) is our potential return. The maximum risk is $4,300 *if* we stay in until expiration and *if* the stock is above $45 a share. As long as the stock doesn't get above $45 and stay above $45 at expiration, we keep the $700 and the risk disappears with the option expiration. To look at it another way, if the stock price goes down by expiration, we make $700; if the stock price stays the same at expiration as it is today, we make $700; even if the stock price goes up $1.49 a share by expiration, we make $700. There are only three ways a stock can go—up, down, or sideways. In our example, we can see that we make money if the stock goes down, we make money if the stock moves sideways, and in this case, we even make money if the stock goes up just as long as it doesn't go up above $45 at expiration.

In that example, we were bearish on the stock and tried to create a spread where we could profit from that bearishness, or even neutrality. If we were bullish on a stock, we could do the same thing with a bullish put spread. Again, we would be opening two legs with the same expiration, and we would be selling a put nearer the money and buying a put further out of the money. As I write, the apparel store company Aeropostale, Inc. (ARO) is bouncing up off a support just above $30. The stock was trading at $31.40 and the $30 puts that expire in 19 days could be sold for $1.20 and the same expiration $25 puts could be bought for about $0.30 so, excluding commission, I could have entered a bullish put spread for a $0.90 a share credit. Using the 10 contract example again, I would have $900 coming into the account as a credit and my risk would be $4,100, at the very worst. That is a potential return on risk of 22 percent in 19 days. As long as the stock stayed above $30 at expiration and I had made no adjustments, I would realize that full return. In this case of a bullish strategy, I make money if the stock price stays the same until expiration and I make money if the stock price goes up. The price can even dip $1.40 a share and I still have realized the full potential. It is only when the stock price falls below $30 that I have any concern and may want to take action. Later in this chapter, I'll look at some actions to take if the stock goes too far in the wrong direction for me.

When I trade these credit spreads, I usually open them with six weeks or less until expiration, and prefer shorter expirations since I want to benefit by the passage of a short amount of time, remembering that the closer to expiration, the faster the time value dissipates. In many cases with approximately a month until expiration, I will find candidates where the potential return on risk approaches 40 percent for the month! These spreads do need some tending. The investor should satisfy himself that a stock on which he considers a bull put spread is actually looking and acting bullish. He is searching for candidates in a bullish market, in a bullish sector that are also looking bullish. If he is considering a bear call spread, he would probably prefer a bearish-looking stock in a bearish sector during a bearish market move. Once he enters the positions, the investor will have to be watchful to be sure there are no signs that the stock, sector, and/or market is reversing because that may be his signal to act.

Is it all worth the time and effort? Well, a potential 1 percent a day or so may be worth examining if you have the time and the inclination. Of course, as always in life, don't count the chickens before they are hatched, and, in the case of spreads, the trade isn't over until the legs are closed by a trade or by expiration. Whipsaws and market turns or news on a stock can require prompt action on the trader's part and some spreads will undoubtedly be losers. As is always the case in the markets, it is critically important to cut losses and let profits run even when trading spreads for monthly income.

So far, we have looked at spreads for bullish situations and spreads for bearish situations. What about equities that are channeling or rolling within a well-defined range? Most of the time, it seems that is what most of them are doing.

PRACTICAL APPLICATION: IRON CONDORS

I have often been entertained and fascinated by some of the great names applied to various trading strategies. In Chapter 7, for example, we'll talk about the joys of "going naked." Here we'll look at another strategy with a great name, the "iron condor." Outside the stock market, a condor is a vulture with a wingspan of about 10 feet. I suspect the strategy name refers to both the width of the spreads involved and the nature of the strategy, which is designed to pick off income in situations where the trader expects the underlying to remain within a range.

The use of the iron condor is a favorite strategy of mine depending on the market and, sometimes, the individual stock. I have often found the strategy to be useful in trading certain index options such as the Russell 2000 (RUT). Index options often offer relatively high premiums and some have European-style options, which means that there can be no exercise until expiration. Though they cannot be assigned until expiration, they are still traded actively until that time. It is also worth noting that with options on indexes, the trader should always check to determine when they expire since they often have a different expiration from options on stocks. Some index options, for example, may expire at the open on the third Friday of the month and, therefore, could not be traded beyond the market close on the day before.

The strategy consists of four option legs that ordinarily are all opened at the same time. In essence, the trader simultaneously opens a bear call spread and a bull put spread and brings in income from both spreads to open the trade. The overall risk, absent any adjustments, is the spread between either the two call strikes or the two put strikes minus the total credit received. Often, these trades have a relatively high likelihood of success.

At the time I am writing, the Russell 2000 is trading around 715. There is a resistance near 750 and a support at 650. As I explained with the bearish call and bullish put spreads, I prefer to sell an out-of-the-money option and buy the next strike that is further out of the money. In that fashion, I am selling nothing but time value and am protecting myself from catastrophic loss in the event of some wild unexpected move. As with the earlier discussions about spreads, when I am making a net sale of time, I usually sell the near month in an effort to get the biggest bang for the buck through rapid deterioration of time value. Using the Russell 2000 example, with 17 days until expiration the following trade was available.

Sell to open the Aug 750 calls (at resistance) and buy to open the Aug 760 calls (as the protective leg) for a credit, before commission, of $1.27 a share and at the same time sell to open the Aug 650 puts and buy to open the Aug 640 puts for an additional credit, before commission, of $0.48. The total credit, therefore, would be $1.75. The spread on the bull put spread and on the bear call spread is each $10. At worst, only one spread could be a loser at expiration since the index price could only be above 750 or below 650 at that time; obviously, it could not be both. The maximum risk, then, is $8.25 for a potential return on risk (before commission) of over 21 percent in just 17 days. As long as the index stays below 750 or above 650 at expiration, there is nothing to do but enjoy the cash. Statistically (based on standard deviation), there was a 78 percent probability that this trade would be profitable.

I do not want to leave the impression that these iron condors can only be used with indexes. Decent iron condor trades can also be found with options on stock as well. On the same day I was looking at the Russell 2000 trade, I also checked out Baidu.com (BIDU), which was trading around $345 a share. It had a resistance around 375 and a support at 275. Again, ignoring commissions, I was looking at selling to open the Aug 380 calls and buying the Aug 390 calls while selling the 320 puts and buying the 310 puts, which were available for an overall credit of about $2.30. In this instance, the statistical probability of achieving a profit was only on the order of 50 percent, but the potential return on risk was a healthy 30 percent for 17 days. These options are American-style so the trader has to be alert for any movement of stock price above the short call or below the short put in order to consider adjustments as we'll discuss in the next section.

Earlier, I ignored commissions as I illustrated some iron condor trades. Commissions are a fact of life and must be considered in actuality. Since the iron condors have four legs, the commission expenses can be fairly high and may increase if the trader closes or adjusts positions during the life of the trade. Some brokers discount commissions on multileg option trades where all the legs are entered at the same time while others may not. Commissions on option trades with full-service brokers may be quite high, even prohibitively so, so always check first to see what your commission cost is going to be; it could influence your decision of whether to trade.

I actually did enter the iron condor I described above on the Russell and will report the final results at the end of this chapter.

ADJUSTING CREDIT SPREADS AND IRON CONDORS

When we are in a bull put spread, everything is wonderful as long as the stock price stays above the strike price of the put we sold. The same is true with a bull call spread as long as the stock price doesn't go above the strike price of the call we sold. However, if the stock price gets above the strike price on our short call or goes below the stock price of our short put, everything can turn from hunky-dory to *Andrea Doria*[*] in very short order. If that situation occurs, the trader should make a decision whether to close both legs of the trade, adjust the trade, or just leave things as they are.

As we saw earlier, the vertical credit spreads have a limited risk equal to the spread between strike prices less the credit received times the number of shares. If we opened a bull put spread on XYZ, for example, in which we sold the 40 puts and bought the 35 puts for a credit of $1, the risk would be $4 a share ($5 spread − $1 credit = $4 a share risk). That is the risk if we hold until expiration, but if there is some time left until expiration, we might be able close the whole spread without suffering the maximum risk.

In the preceding case, we would be in no danger of being put shares (assigned the stock) unless the stock price were to fall below $40. If it did, that should trigger an evaluation on our part. While immediate action may not be necessary, we should determine how much time is left until expiration, what it would cost to simply close both legs of the trade, and how

---

[*]For those too young to remember, the *Andrea Doria* was a passenger ship that capsized and sank after a collision with the *Stockholm* in 1956.

bearish the price dip may be. If the stock price dropped about the amount of the quarterly dividend on the ex-dividend day, we probably would have expected the dip and it would not necessarily suggest bearishness. On the other hand, if some bad news about the company were released and the price dropped on high volume there would be a serious suggestion of bearishness and we would then look at choices available to us.

The first consideration would simply be to see what it would cost to close the whole trade. Next, we would see what it would cost to buy to close the short leg ($40 put we sold to start the trade). Almost surely, we would sustain a loss on that specific leg if we bought back the short leg, but we would still own the long leg ($35 put in our example). Assuming that there is some time left, we might choose that action since the price for that $35 put would be expected to increase as the stock price continued to drop so we could take a loss on closing the short leg, but would still be gaining on the long leg if the stock kept moving down and there was enough time left.

If our options are close to expiration, we may just want to buy to close the $40 put leg. Depending on the stock price and time to expiration, we can still profit overall. As an example, suppose it was expiration Friday and the stock price dipped to $39.60. There would only be 40 cents intrinsic value in the $40 put and hardly any time value so we might be able to buy to close that leg for 70 or 75 cents. Our long $35 put probably would have no value so we would just let it expire worthless. Our overall profit would be about 75 cents (the $1.50 credit the market paid us when we entered the trade minus the 75 cents we paid to close the short leg).

As a matter of practicality, many times, if I am in a bull put spread and the stock price runs up so that I can buy to close the short leg cheap enough to capture a decent profit (50 percent of the potential or more), I'll do just that and hang onto the long position. Now I own the long position for nothing and if the stock price then turns back down with some time left, the long position can regain value, which just adds profit to an already successful trade.

All the same principles apply to the bear call spread. If the stock price goes above the strike of the call we sold, we need to examine what is going on and then go through essentially the same process I just described for the puts. Only, in this case, we would consider closing the whole trade or only closing the short call leg depending on time until expiration and what it looks like the stock price is doing.

Similar though not identical analysis can be applied to adjusting iron condors. A major difference between the vertical credit spreads and iron condors is that a credit spread can become quite profitable to close if the stock price takes off in a desired direction. If we hold a bearish call spread and the bottom drops out of the stock, we are probably in good shape and can close out just the short call leg and guarantee a great profit in the trade. When we are in a bear call spread, the only danger is up. However, if we are in an iron condor and have that same bear call spread, we also would have a bull put spread so a precipitous price drop could put us at risk for loss on the down side as could a precipitous rise put us in danger on the call side. With an iron condor in place, we need the stock price to trade in a range between our short call and our short put legs. Since there is danger both above and below, we have to consider the possibility of a whipsaw if we start adjusting iron condors. If our condor is created using American-style options (like most stocks), I have to be aware of the possibility of assignment of calls if the stock goes above my short call strike or if it falls below my short put strike. In the case of European-style options, I do not have that concern until expiration. For that reason, I do prefer European-style options when trading iron condors.

As a practical matter, if I have opened an iron condor and the price of the underlying (stock or index) begins to run in one direction, I will watch the price of the short option in the other direction as well as the short option in the direction of the move. That is, if an index is moving up, I will follow the price of the put I sold to see if I can buy it back cheaply; if the index is moving down sharply, I'll watch to see if I can take major profit by buying back the short call. If I can get rid of both the short legs at profits as the price moves up and down, I may wind up with a locked-in profit and still be holding a long strangle (both a long call and a long put of different strikes) that has essentially no cost and offers profit potential in either direction. Since the short legs are both gone, I no longer have any risk of assignment.

 GETTING INTO GEAR

It has often been said that most option traders lose, and most lose because they buy short-term out-of-the-money options. If traders are losing most of the time following a strategy, it has always seemed to me that I can profit by doing just the opposite.

In this chapter we looked at some income-producing strategies that are designed to accomplish that very task. We have looked at short-term strategies designed to profit in bullish markets, in bearish markets, and in range-bound markets. Once we have determined market action, we can set our plan to work. If things look bullish, we can consider a bullish put spread; if things look bearish, we can go to a bear call spread; and, if things look neutral we can see if we can find an iron condor we like.

Each of those strategies can produce quite a hefty monthly return, and all of them can do so with precisely limited risk. Granted, it does take a little extra time to monitor and, sometimes adjust these positions, but with potential returns on risk of 20 percent to 30 percent a month, the effort may well be worth it.

In Chapter 7, we'll explore some riskier strategies that can bring in spectacular returns if you like the idea of being naked.

Incidentally, I promised to tell you how the iron condor trade that I placed on the Russell 2000 (RUT) with 17 days until expiration went. I lost my shirt and had to turn to writing books. No, just kidding. . . . I stayed in the trade for four days and closed all legs for a net gain before commission of 9.7 percent.

CHAPTER 7

Playing Naked

Income with No Investment

T hink, for a moment, how insurance companies operate. They are paid handsome premiums to take a risk. If they insure your home against fire damage they are paid up front to take the risk that they will have to pay you if your home catches fire. If your home doesn't catch fire before the policy expires, they just keep your premium and charge you another one for the next time period. When they write a policy, they take on a contingent obligation, and if the contingency doesn't occur, they keep the premium. As we all know, a lot of insurance companies have become extremely successful using this method.

What do insurance companies have to do with taking our clothes off? Absolutely nothing, but their business plan is analogous to going naked in the market. For the options trader, going naked should not conjure up a mental picture of someone sitting in their office with no clothes on while trading options. It simply means that there is no underlying security position or that the position is not hedged from market risk. In Chapter 6, we looked at some spreads, and in each of the strategies we examined, the risk was hedged by another option leg. When we sell naked options, there is no second leg nor is there an underlying security position as there would be if we were selling covered calls against a stock we owned.

When we sell naked options (puts or calls) we take in a premium to open the position, and in exchange for the premium we are paid, we are undertaking an obligation; we take on risk. As we'll see, the risks can be very significant as can the rewards, if we can set up positions so that we have a two out of three (sometimes three out of three) chance to profit. There is a significant difference in the potential dollar risk between selling naked puts and selling naked calls, which we'll examine a little later in this chapter. However, you may be pleasantly surprised when you compare the risk of selling naked options to the risk of stock ownership, alone, and to certain other strategies that are considered to be relatively safe.

Though your broker will have certain requirements to permit you to sell naked options, once they are met you will be able to generate regular income with no investment.

SELLING NAKED PUTS

The Benefits

Selling naked puts is one of my favorite income-producing strategies in a bullish market. Later in this chapter, I'll set out my personal trading rules, but first we'll examine the mechanics of the strategy along with its benefits and risks. Whenever we sell an option, we take on an obligation. When we sell puts, we obligate ourselves to buy shares of stock at a specific price (the strike price we have sold) at any time before the option expires, and, in exchange for undertaking that obligation, we are paid a premium. The premium goes into our account the day after our order to sell the puts is filled. Since option contracts ordinarily control 100 shares of stock, our obligation would be to buy 100 shares of the stock for each contract we sell.

As an example, suppose the shares of XYZ are trading for $61 a share and the $60 put options that expire in four weeks can be sold for $2 a share. We decide to sell 10 contracts of those $60 puts, which will bring $2,000 (less commission) into our account the following day. No matter what, that $2,000 is ours to keep. Now, in exchange for that $2,000, we have agreed to buy 1,000 shares of XYZ at $60 a share anytime between the time we enter the position and when it expires in a month. Is there any risk that the puts will be exercised and we will have to buy the stock if the share price remains around the $61 mark where it was when we sold the puts? No, because whoever bought the puts could sell his stock on the open market for $61 a share so why would he want to exercise his puts and force us to buy it at $60? If we were assigned when the stock price was at $61, we would be obligated to buy the shares for $60, but could immediately sell them at $61 and make another $1 a share on the transaction. If the stock price increased from $61 would there be any danger that the puts would be exercised? Again, the answer is no since the put buyer could sell his stock for more on the open market than he would get by forcing us to buy at $60 a share. Now we can see that if the stock price stayed the same or if it went up, we would win. Obviously, a stock price can only go up, down, or sideways so in our example we can see that we make money if the stock price stays the same or goes up. That means we make money in two of the three possible scenarios.

Wait, though: What happens if the stock goes down to $60.05? Again, it is extremely unlikely that it would be assigned so we also make money even if the stock price goes down, but does not drop below the strike price of the puts we sold. Suppose, though, that the stock dropped to $58.50 and we were still short our $60 puts. In that case, we would be assigned the 1,000 shares of stock at $60, but what would our real cost be? Remember, the market actually paid us $2 a share to take on the risk that the stock could be assigned to us at $60. Now, when the stock is assigned at $60, we are only paying $58 because we got the $2 up front. Now, we own the stock at $58 a share and could immediately sell it at $58.50. As you can see, commissions aside, even if the stock dropped to $58 we would be in a breakeven situation when we bought it for $60 because we were paid $2 to take the risk in the first place.

Though I generally use the strategy to produce income, some investors sell naked puts with the specific intent of having the stock put sold to them because it can be a way to buy stocks at "wholesale." In the preceding example, if we liked the stock at $60 a share, we would probably like it even better if we could buy it for $58 when it is trading at $60. With the stock at $61, we would do the same thing and sell the $60 naked puts for $2. If the price dropped to around $60 and we were assigned the stock, we would have a basis of $58 and we could then hold the stock for dividends and/or price appreciation and we could sell covered calls as well. The stock would be ours, but at the wholesale price of $58 rather than for the $60 we were willing to pay.

The Risks

I have always been amused by brokers who identify the strategy of selling naked puts as being quite risky while at the same time urging us to buy stocks. Using the example in the previous section, which is riskier, buying the stock for $60 or buying the same stock for $58 after the market has paid you $2 a share to buy it at $60? The risk in buying a stock is that it can go to zero and while that is not common, it does happen. Witness the downfall of companies like Lehman Brothers, Bear Stearns, and Washington Mutual as examples of the serious risks that attend stock ownership. If I sell a naked put and am assigned the stock, what have I done? I have bought a stock. However, before I bought the stock, I was paid a premium to take a risk to buy the stock. In either case, I have bought the stock and the risk is the net cost of the stock. If I pay full price for the stock, my risk is greater than if I pay full price less a premium the market has given me in the first place. The premium I received reduces my overall risk.

Curiously, brokers will tell you that selling naked puts is risky but that writing covered calls is relatively safe. The truth is that the risk graph is the same for selling covered calls as it is for selling naked puts. If we buy a stock and write an at-the-money covered call as we discussed in Chapter 4, our risk is the price we paid for the stock minus what we are paid for selling the call. If we bought the stock for $60 a share and sold a $60 covered call for $2, our risk is $58. So, too, if we sell a $60 put for $2 and the stock is put to us, our risk is $58. It is the same in both situations. In each case, the downside is unlimited down to zero; that is the risk. However, in order to write covered calls, we need to own the stock in the first place and must actually invest the capital to buy the shares. When selling naked puts we don't own anything; we are only being paid to take the risk that we might have to buy the stock at a predetermined price.

In all events, ownership of the stock, alone, has greater risk than being assigned the stock after receiving a premium for selling the naked puts or than owning the stock and receiving a premium for selling a covered call. In fact, little is riskier than simply owning a stock so why do brokers push stock ownership and tell you that selling naked puts is so risky? The question really is: riskier for whom? Is it your interests that concern them, or is it their own risk that worries them?

I suggest that brokers want to dissuade us from selling naked puts because they perceive a risk to themselves. It goes back to the market crash in 1987. Before the crash, selling in-the-money naked puts had become a popular strategy. As long as stocks were going up, the puts were not being assigned and naked put sellers were generating a steady stream of income. When the market crashed and many brokers simply refused to answer their phones, a whole lot of stock was assigned to the put sellers and many could not afford to pay for it so the brokers were stuck. It turned out that selling naked puts had been very risky to brokers so now they tell you what a risky strategy it is while encouraging you to buy stock. The truth is your risk is less when you sell a naked put and are assigned stock at your strike price than it would be if you just bought the stock at the strike price without capturing the premium.

As is always the case when buying stock, whether we buy it straight out or are assigned the stock, our risk is the net cost of the stock. So our risk in selling naked puts is that we may be assigned the stock and we would then simply have the normal risk associated with stock ownership.

My Rules for Selling Naked Puts

When I sell naked puts as I often do, I am selling them to bring in income and not to buy the stock at wholesale. Since I trade the strategy for income, I try to avoid situations where it looks like there may be a serious likelihood that the stock will be assigned. In other words, I try to enter the trade with some edge that can help me achieve my goal. The following are my personal rules for selling naked puts:

- Use the strategy when the market, sector, and stock are bullish. (Sometimes, I'll settle for just the sector and stock if the sector is moving up strongly even if the overall market is down. An example of that was in mid-2008 when oil and energy were strong and the rest of the market was falling.)
- Only sell out-of-the-money puts at the strike price immediately below either a price support or a trend support as the stock price bounces off that support.
- Sell puts that will expire shortly—a week to a maximum of five or six weeks to expiration.
- Only sell naked puts on stock of companies I like and consider to be fundamentally sound because I may wind up owning them.
- Make sure that I wouldn't mind owning the stock at the price of the strike I am selling.
- Be sure that I have enough cash (or cash and margin) in my account to buy the stock in the event it is assigned to me.
- Check to see whether there is an earnings announcement between the time I enter the position and expiration and if there is be sure to exit before the announcement.

Even though my intent in using the strategy is to bring in income, I need to have a plan in the event the stock price drops and my put goes in the money.

Adjustments and Exits for Naked Puts

Since I only sell out-of-the-money naked puts, I run almost no risk of assignment unless the stock price falls and my put goes in the money. Once that happens, I am at risk of assignment and that assignment can occur at any time before expiration (with American-style options). Normally, we would not expect early assignment as long as the option still had some time value in addition to the intrinsic value. As long as there is time value, the owner of the put could simply sell it and be paid both the intrinsic value and the time value. If he just exercised the put, he would lose the time value and get only the intrinsic value. As an example, suppose a trader owns 1,000 shares of XYZ and 10 contracts of the Oct 60 puts on XYZ. The stock drops to $59 a share with three weeks until the put would expire. The Oct 60 put is trading at $1.75. The intrinsic value of the put is $1 and the time value is $0.75. If the trader were to exercise his put and assign his stock, he would sell the stock for $60 and gain the $1 of intrinsic (in-the-money) value, but he would not get the extra $0.75 a share for the time. He would sell his 1,000 shares for $60,000. However, if he sold the puts at $1.75 he would bring in $1,750 for his 10 contracts and could sell his stock for the $59 market price to bring in $59,000. Now he would have a total of $60,750 instead of the $60,000 for just exercising his puts.

Even though it makes more sense for the put owner to sell the put than it does to sell his stock even if the put still has time value that does not mean that everyone will follow that course. Many years ago, I had sold some naked puts and a couple of days later, the stock price dropped just a little below the strike price I had sold, but there was quite a lot of time left so I thought I had no concern about early assignment at that point. There was plenty of time value in the option, but to my great surprise the next morning my broker phoned and advised I had been put the stock. Someone who owned puts pushed the panic button and I was assigned the shares. While it didn't make financial sense, it happened and has made me aware that it can always occur. This experience happened early in my trading back in the roaring bull market of the late 1990s and, as fate would have it, the same day I received notification that the stock had been assigned to me, it gapped up on the open a couple of dollars and I not only got to keep the premium for selling the puts in the first place, I also made a nice quick profit by selling the stock that had been put to me. Luck can definitely play a part as it did in those circumstances.

Of greater concern when trading naked puts for income (as opposed to using them to buy stock wholesale) is what to do when the stock price goes into the money.

Stop, Drop, or Roll   As we have seen, once a put goes in the money there is a concern that the stock may be assigned. As a result of the experience I related above I tend to react quickly to a situation where the stock price breaks down through support (and/or my naked put goes in the money). There are a number of possible actions that can be taken and, for me, what I do depends on the then current price of the puts, the time until expiration, and where the next level of support lies.

First, I stop and consider the whole situation. If I find that I can buy back the put I sold for less than the premium I received to open the position, I do that and close (or drop) the position at a profit. Similarly, if there is not another support close below the current stock price I also may decide just to close the position even if at a loss. However, I have some other alternatives as well.

If the stock is near the next support level down, I may decide to roll my position out to the next expiration or even roll it out to the next expiration and down a strike price (or more than one strike price). When I say roll, I am referring to a trade where I simultaneously buy to close the original position and sell to open a new position in a later month and/or to a different strike price. Just rolling out a month will bring in additional premium since an extra month until expiration means an extra month of time value. Going back to the example of selling a $60 put on XYZ that we have been using in this chapter, we can see that whatever the premium for the put that expires this month may be, the premium for the same strike next month will be more since there is more time.

Suppose I have sold the Oct 60 put on XYZ and as it nears expiration on the third Friday of October the stock price has fallen to $59.80 and is dealing with a support around the $60 mark. If I do nothing and the stock price is $59.80, I am going to be assigned the stock at expiration for $60 a share. At $59.80, there is 20 cents of intrinsic value and as we get closer and closer to expiration, the time value diminishes more and more rapidly. Suppose the time value gets down to 20 cents a day or so before expiration. Now the premium to buy to close my put would be 40 cents (20 cents intrinsic value and 20 cents time value). The premium for the next month $60 put would be more since there is still the same 20 cents intrinsic value, but there is much more time value. Let's say the time value for that extra month is 80 cents so the premium for the November $60 puts would be $1 (20 cents intrinsic plus 80 cents time). I could roll from the Oct 60 puts to the Nov 60 puts for a net credit before commission of 60 cents. To break the roll down, I would buy to close the October $60 puts for 40 cents and simultaneously sell to open the November $60 puts for $1. The sale of the November puts would pay for closing the October position and still give me an additional credit of 60 cents. By rolling out in this situation, I would have added cash to my account.

What if the stock price has dropped well below my strike price? Of course, I have the option of just closing the position and taking my lumps or I could try to make some lemonade out of those lemons. I could roll both out and down. In that scenario, I would buy to close the current position and simultaneously sell to open the next expiration out and a strike (or more) down. Using the same example of the October $60 puts, I could roll out to November as we just saw and also roll down to sell a lower strike price. We have already seen how rolling out brings in more time value, and now, by rolling to a lower strike price we can reduce the risk of assignment by selling a new strike price below the next support level down. For example, suppose that the stock was trading at $61 a share when we sold the slightly out-of-the-money October $60 put and that we got $2 when we opened the trade. Now, suppose the stock drops to $56 a share. If we rolled down to sell the $55 put, we might expect to get $2 for selling that also slightly out-of-the-money put as well. Under these circumstances, we might not want to make that roll since our October puts are already $4 in-the-money and it would cost us a debit to roll out only a month and down a strike. We could check, however, and find a further out expiration where the $55 strike was commanding enough premium to bring us a credit over-all. Frankly, in that situation, I would have to be very bullish on the stock to roll very far out in time since the ability to roll out eventually vanishes when there are no further out expirations to which to roll. Sometimes it is just better to eat the loss and move on to the next trade.

Requirements to Sell Naked Puts

As you might suspect from the discussion about risks of selling naked puts, some brokers are beyond nervous about letting the retail trader engage in the strategy. If this is a strategy that appeals to you, I suggest you check with brokers before opening an account to see what their specific require-ments may be as they can change radically from firm to firm. Some broker-ages simply do not permit clients to sell naked puts. My advice is to avoid those firms. It's your money and you are the one taking the risk and as we have seen, that is no greater than the risk of buying a stock. What right does someone you employ have to tell you that you are not allowed to place your money at risk as you choose? I don't mean you should blindly sell naked puts without understanding the strategy completely and without practic-ing it before you put yourself at risk. Instead, if you are going to trade the strategy, learn it first. Most brokerages do require that you have knowledge or at least attest that you have experience with the strategy before autho-rizing your account to sell naked puts. That requirement is universal and only makes good sense. You'll note that I wrote brokerage firms require that "you at least attest" that you have trading experience. There is no test and anyone could lie on their application. From the broker's perspective, the client has signed a document where the trader has said he has the trad-ing experience. If he has lied, he has only hurt himself and the broker can use the client's false statement in defense if he is later sued and the client claims his losses are the broker's fault. The point is the broker is protecting himself and the client should be honest for if he hasn't learned a strategy he is trading, he will, in all likelihood, be doomed to failure.

In addition to the experience requirement, brokerages also require certain minimums in the account before allowing a client to trade naked options. Depending on how much a given firm wants to encourage or discourage clients who trade naked options, the minimum account size can range from about $2,000 to $100,000 or more. It seems obvious that we should not be selling naked puts if we have a $500 or $1,000 account since we probably don't have enough to buy shares if they are assigned. A single contract (controlling 100 shares) on a $10 stock would require the whole account to buy the shares and would literally put everything at risk. Any theory of diversification or money management is out the window if we put all our account eggs in one basket.

Another important requirement when selling naked puts is the margin requirement. I began this chapter discussing the concept of generating income with no investment and that is one of the beautiful things about selling naked puts in the right circumstances. We are paid a premium to take a known risk for a limited period of time and if we are selling out-of-the-money puts we are assured of keeping the whole premium less commission as long as the stock price stays the same or has gone up by the time we have reached expiration (and we have made no adjustment in the meantime). Though we have made no investment, money will be put on hold in our account as long as we are short the put. It is very important that you check with your broker to determine what their margin requirements are on the sale of naked puts because, again, we can find a large variation from broker to broker. The margin is "marked to market," which means it changes from day to day depending on price movement.

In general, as a rule of thumb we can expect roughly 25 percent to 30 percent of the position will be kept on hold for the duration of the trade. A standard calculation to determine what will be kept on hold follows.

Twenty-five percent of the market price of the underlying + the premium received − any out-of-the-money amount *or* 10 percent of the market price of the underlying + the premium *whichever is greater.*

As an example using the calculation, suppose XYZ is trading at $61 and we sell 10 contracts of the $60 puts for $2. The value of the underlying is $61,000 ($61 a share × 1,000 shares) so 25 percent of that is $15,250 and the premium was $2,000 (10 contracts × 100 shares per contract × $2 a share) for a total of $17,250 and since the strike sold is $1 out of the money minus $1,000 for a total on hold of $16,250. The alternative calculation is $6,100 (10 percent of $61,000) plus the $2,000 premium for a total of $8,100. Since $16,250 is greater than $8,100, the $16,250 would be on hold in the account until the position is closed.

Again, it is critical to understand that every broker may have a different calculation so check directly with them before opening a position and remember the margin will change from day to day.

For What Category of Investor Is the Naked Put Strategy Suitable?

Selling naked puts does open the investor to the risk of being assigned stock he is obligated to buy so it seems clear that the investor considering the strategy must be able to afford to fulfill his agreement if the stock is put to him. He needs to have some assets in place before adding this part to his money machine. In other words, the strategy is not for someone who has a small account. Our friend, Forrest Footloose, should probably look for another strategy unless he has already accumulated some assets.

Naked short put positions also need to be monitored and relatively quick decisions occasionally need to be made when a short put goes into the money. That means the investor has to have the time to monitor his positions and decide when and whether to close or adjust a position. That may or may not work for folks like the Middletons who are so busy with kids and jobs that they just don't have the time. I don't mean to suggest that monitoring these positions is terribly time-consuming, but I do mean to suggest that it is not wise to ignore them once in place. Time will also be required to learn the strategy well and to practice paper trading before taking on real money risk. In Chapter 6, I'll discuss important differences between paper trading and real money trading, but I do believe paper trading is a worthwhile exercise to arrive at an in-depth understanding of any strategy. Once again, the individual will need to balance time demands against the desirability of learning and using any strategy.

Ed Balding, the last of our hypothetical investors, may be the most likely to have the existing assets and time necessary to devote to the strategy. For investors like Ed, the biggest factor may be assessment of risk of additional stock ownership along with an analysis of time he is willing to devote to the strategy.

In my own investing, I have found that selling naked puts can be very lucrative. It does require study and understanding beyond the knowledge of the average retail trader and should not be entered lightly, but the income this strategy produces in the right markets has made it worthwhile for me.

SELLING NAKED CALLS

The Risks

I began the section on naked puts by discussing the benefits. As we examine selling naked calls, I have chosen to address the risks first because they are very significant. From a theoretical viewpoint, at least, they are potentially unlimited. Naked puts, you will recall, entail a risk that the stock could be put to us and our risk is then limited to the net price we pay for the stock *if* it is assigned to us. Since a stock price can't go below zero, the most we can lose is our whole investment. That is not the case with selling naked calls. When we sell a naked call we are obligating ourselves to deliver the stock at the strike price we have sold if called anytime before expiration. By definition, we don't own the stock in the first place so if our position is called, we would have to buy the stock at the market price in order to fulfill our obligation to sell it at the strike price. Suppose we sold 10 contracts of the slightly out-of-the-money $60 naked calls on XYZ for $2 a share when the stock was trading at $59. As long as the stock stays below $60, we have no problem. However, suppose that one afternoon, after market close, XYZ announces the creation of a product that is ready for market and which will enhance longevity at a relatively small cost per person or suppose they announce they have discovered the cure for all cancers. What is likely to happen to the stock price the next morning? In all probability it will gap up at the open and rocket from there. Yesterday it was a $59 stock and today it opened at $300 and has climbed to $360 a share. The effect on us is devastating. Assuming we are assigned on our short call position, we would have to buy 1,000 shares of stock at $360 a share ($360,000) so that we could sell it at $60 a share for a nice quick $300,000 kick in the pants.

Obviously, that scenario is extremely unlikely, but it is used to illustrate the dangers inherent in selling naked calls. A real-life example can be seen with Google (GOOG). On April 17, 2008, it closed down almost $5.50 at $449.54 a share. Suppose I had sold the May 475 calls sometime during that day. The next morning the stock gapped up to open at $535.21, a 60-point jump and from there it continued to soar, closing the month of April at $593.08. Whether I bought back to close the calls I had sold or whether I was called out, the loss would be no less than $60 a share—overnight!

Make no mistake, selling naked calls can be very risky, riskier in terms of dollars than selling naked puts. Rarely, I do sell naked calls, but as you will see by my personal rules for selling naked calls, I make serious efforts to try to avoid large losses. As you'll see, I'll usually create a hedge in the form of a wide vertical spread to at least place a limit on the potential loss.

Benefits of Selling Naked Calls

While selling naked puts is one of my favorite strategies, selling naked calls isn't. However, it does have the advantage of establishing an income stream during bearish moves of market, sector, and/or stock. In essence, the benefits are much the same as I detailed in the section on selling naked puts. There is no cash investment; the trader who sells out-of-the-money calls will profit two out of three ways (if the stock price goes down or stays the same); and the trade will ultimately benefit from the passage of time. Nevertheless, the risks attendant to a "black swan" move (one that is highly improbable such as a move greater than two standard deviations) find me employing this strategy much less often than selling puts. Instead, if I see a position that looks good for selling naked calls, I'll sell a call that is just above a trend or price resistance and then as protection against catastrophe, I'll buy a way out-of-the-money call for a low premium just to put a lid on the worst-case scenario.

As an example, back in the late summer of 2008, Qualcom (QCOM) was trading just below a resistance at $55 a share. With about a month to expiration, the Sept 55 call was selling for $1.95. While the play looked good, I have seen QCOM make some pretty wild jumps over the years so I looked to see what cheap protection against abject catastrophe might be available. The Sept 65 calls were available for 9 cents and if used in a spread, I could sell the Sept 55s for $1.95 and buy the Sept 65s for 9 cents, thereby bringing in $1.86 a share, but instead of having unlimited risk at $1.95, I would have only $8.14 ($10 spread less $1.86 credit upon entry) risk and still bring in $1.86. While I did not make this trade myself, it is an illustration of a way to effectively sell a call, gain almost the same premium as if the call were naked, yet put a cap on the risk.

My Rules for Selling Naked Calls

- Ask myself if I am really sure I want to take unlimited risk.
- Use the strategy only when the market, sector, and specific stock are all bearish.
- Do not use the strategy on stocks that have had a tendency to be volatile; instead use companies that are in relatively boring industries where exciting announcements are unlikely (like a cereal company).
- Only sell out-of-the-money calls at the strike price immediately above either a price or trend resistance as the stock price bounces away from that support.
- Sell calls that will expire shortly (a week to no more than a month at most).
- Consider creating a wide spread by buying a far out-of-the-money call to create a limit on potential loss (usually choose this alternative).
- Check to see whether there is an earnings announcement between the time I enter the position and expiration and if there is be sure to exit before the announcement.
- Watch the trade like a hawk; have a stop to buy to close the position contingent on a stock price and have an alert in place to warn as the stock price approaches the level where I would want to close the trade.

Requirements for Selling Naked Calls

Here, again, brokerage firms will differ markedly in their requirements, but, in general, selling naked calls requires approval at the highest level by most, if not all firms. Minimum account size and trading experience will probably be required before the trader is authorized to sell naked calls. The only way I know to determine what the requirements are is to ask.

As in the case of selling naked puts, there are margin requirements for selling naked calls and, as with puts, they are marked to market and change from day to day with price movement in the markets. Once again, it is the investor's responsibility to check with his broker to find exactly what they are.

For What Category Investor Is the Naked Call Strategy Suitable?

Though I have emphasized the risks of selling naked calls, I do not mean to scare everyone away from this strategy. It does bring in income and it can be very effective under the right market conditions. As with all strategies, it is critically important to understand the risks before ever entering a trade and selling naked calls can be risky.

The strategy is definitely not for everyone, but it can be for the right trading personality equipped with knowledge of the strategy. As you have no doubt gathered by now, selling naked calls requires someone who is willing to take risk in exchange for a stream of income. It is for traders who want to continue an income stream even when stocks and markets are bearish. It is not for the timid. When considering use of the strategy, it is important to consider the "how do I sleep" category. All of us handle risk differently and we need to evaluate whether we can sleep soundly while using any given strategy. Selling naked calls can approach the outer edges of risk so it is a strategy that should be undertaken only if the trader is comfortable with the risk and knows absolutely that he will react immediately if his exit is hit. This is not a place to have an internal discussion whether to hang in a while longer to see if the stock will turn back down; it is a place to have a predetermined exit and act if it is hit.

Naked option trades need to be monitored closely and, if anything, a naked short call position needs to monitored even more closely than a naked short put position.

COMBINING THE STRATEGIES—NAKED STRADDLES AND NAKED STRANGLES

When we perceive that the market, sector, and stock are all relatively neutral as they can be much of the time, we might consider selling naked straddles or naked strangles. In creating a naked straddle, we sell both a naked put and a naked call with the same strike price. The naked strangle is placed when we sell naked puts and naked calls, but with differing strike prices.

From what we have already seen, by selling both the put and the call options we can expect to take in a relatively large amount of time value when we open the trade. However, the maximum profit is limited to what we take in when we open the positions and that limited profit comes with a large potential risk. The risk is somewhat counterbalanced by the fact that the probability of actually making a profit is often quite high. Essentially, these trades are designed for situations where there is not a lot of volatility. A quiet market, sector, and/or stock can provide the right circumstances for these strategies.

Naked Straddle

Once we have identified a candidate that appears to be trading in a range or where the volatility is dropping or appears relatively stable, we can explore the naked straddle. In this play, we are selling both the calls and the puts with an at-the-money strike price. Since we are selling both options, we will be bringing in two premiums and since both are approximately at the money, we can expect that most, if not all, the premium will be for time value. The objective is to keep as much of the initial credit as possible at expiration or if we exit the position early. As I noted in the introductory section, the maximum potential is whatever credit we obtain at the outset.

We can easily calculate the breakevens on the upside and on the down-side at expiration. Suppose XYZ is trading at $60 and we sell the Oct 60 calls for $5 and the Oct 60 puts for $4. Ignoring commissions for the example, we would take in $9. To establish the breakevens at expiration, we would subtract $9 from the $60 strike price to get a downside breakeven of $51 and we would add the $9 to the $60 strike price to get an upside breakeven of $69. If the stock price falls anywhere between $51 and $69 we will have a profit at expiration. You can see that if the stock went to $69 at expiration, it has $9 of intrinsic value and it would cost us the $9 we received as an initial credit to buy to close the call leg. The put leg would have no value and would expire worthless. On the other hand, if the stock was trading at $51 at expiration, the $60 put would be $9 in the money and it would cost us $9 to buy to close our put position. Anywhere between the $51 mark and $69, there would be some profit. The maximum profit only would be real-ized if the stock closed exactly at $60 at expiration so chances are slim that we would ever enjoy that circumstance. In that event, both the 60 put and the 60 call that we sold to open the trade would expire worthless and we would keep the whole $9 credit with which we started the trade. However, that does not mean we necessarily should avoid these trades. What if the price closed somewhere in between the $51 and the $69? Let's assume it closed at $66 at expiration. We originally got the $9 credit, but now the $60 calls are $6 in the money so we would have to buy to close that leg for $6.

The put leg would have no value so we would not need to do anything with it so the trade would have a profit of $3 (initial $9 credit minus $6 to close the call leg). Similarly, suppose the stock closed at $53 at expiration. Now we could have a $2 gain for the trade. In that case, the puts would be $7 in the money and we would buy to close that position for $7 and have $2 of our original credit left over.

The relatively wide spread between breakevens can lead to some high probabilities that these trades will be profitable, but the risk can be quite high. Once outside the breakevens, the theoretical losses can be unlimited if no adjustments are made. Since we are naked puts, if the stock goes in the tank, we could put the stock at $60 and run the risk that the price could go to zero. If the stock ran above $69, the theoretical risk would be unlimited since we could be called out at $60 and would have to buy the stock at whatever price it reached in order to sell it at $60. Since there is such high risk, the trader, as always, should have an exit plan in place before ever entering the trade. There are a couple of alternatives the trader might consider so the trade doesn't get away too far.

Adjusting Naked Straddles My first choice is to simply close the whole trade (buying to close the call position and the put position) if the stock price hits a breakeven. Unless the stock has become more volatile, if the options are nearing expiration, there should be little time value left so I would not expect to have to pay much more than the initial credit to get out of a situation that could become dangerous quickly. We could also trade the play a little more dynamically if we choose. For example, when the stock price made a directional move and then turned, we could buy to close the out-of-the-money leg for a profit and await the next turn to buy to close the other leg. To add some clarity to the example, suppose we sold the $60 puts and $60 calls on XYZ when it was trading at $60 for the same $4 and $5 as in the previous section. Then suppose the stock price dipped to $54 and turned back up. Since they would now be somewhat deep in the money, the puts would have more value because of the drop in stock price and the calls would have lost value. At that point, we could buy to close the calls and realize a profit on that leg. Now, we'll say the stock runs up to $63 and turns down. It is quite likely that the puts will have declined substantially in price so we could now buy to close that leg at a profit as well and we would then be out of the trade having achieved a profit on each leg.

Another possible plan would be to leg out by buying to close the leg that is in the money and has hit the breakeven. That method avoids paying to close the other leg but still does leave the trader naked the other leg. In our earlier example, if the stock went to $69, we might close the call leg and just leave the put leg in place if we had reason to believe the stock would stay above $51 until expiration. In choosing this alternative, we would save the small cost of buying to close the way out-of-the-money put and the commission we would incur on that transaction, but we would still have the risk inherent in any naked put position.

Yet another alternative would be to add a protective leg in whatever direction the stock was moving and while that would serve to limit risk on the leg, it would cost an additional premium and commission.

Naked Strangles

When we consider naked strangles, as in the case of the naked straddles, we seek candidates exhibiting relatively low volatility; we like to see securities that are trading in a range. Instead of selling puts and calls with the same strike price as in the case of the straddles, we look to sell two different strike prices with the same expiration. Ordinarily, we sell out-of-the-money puts and calls to create the naked strangle. I prefer to sell calls that are just above a resistance and puts that are just below support. In selling these out-of-the-money options, I am paid a time value premium for each, but since they are out of the money and not at the money, I would not take in as much as I would selling the at-the-money options as we do with straddles. In exchange for accepting a smaller total premium, we get a wider breakeven and a wider range over which we will be able to keep the whole initial credit. Statistically, we can also expect to have a greater likelihood that the trade will be profitable because the breakevens are more widely spread.

Going back to our example with XYZ at $60, I might decide to sell the Oct $65 calls and the Oct $55 puts. Suppose the calls are going for $1.75 and the puts for $1.25. The net credit before commission would be $3 and as long as the stock was between $55 and $65 at expiration, I would be able to keep the whole credit. Breakevens are even a little wider apart. Again, ignoring commissions, they would be at $52 and $68, respectively. As you can see, if, for example, the stock dropped to $52 at expiration, my $55 puts would be $3 in the money and it would cost me that intrinsic value to buy to close the put position. So, too, if the stock price was at $68 at expiration, the calls would be $3 in the money and it would cost $3 in intrinsic value to buy to close that leg.

Once again, since both legs are naked, there is a high risk once the breakeven is passed. Here, again, the risk is to zero on the put side and unlimited on the call side so the trader will need to have a plan to close or adjust his position just in case the stock price enters a danger zone.

Adjusting Naked Strangles   When selling a naked strangle, both the puts we sell and the calls we sell are generally out of the money. In addition, I try to establish a little additional protection for myself by selling calls that are above a resistance and puts that are below a support. Though there is never any guarantee that either a support or a resistance will hold, the stock price has turned back at each of those levels in the past so there is some expectancy that those supports and resistances will hold again. If one does not hold, I would take action. There are a couple of alternatives from which to choose. I could simply close the whole trade by buying to close both legs and, in that event, would probably profit on one leg and take a loss on the other. If the stock price had declined, I would probably have a gain on the call side and a loss on the put side and vice versa if the stock price had gone up. Another alternative would be to buy to close the put leg if the stock closed below support or buy to close the call side if the stock closed above resistance. In the example in the last section, I sold the $55 put and the $65 call. If we assume that the stock had been trading in a channel between $56 and $63, those levels would be support and resistance, respectively. On a close below $56, I would buy to close the put leg or on a break above $63, I would buy to close the call leg. On the break below support or above resistance, the option would still be out of the money (absent some large gap move) so I still would be buying back nothing but time value to close the position. Depending on how much time had elapsed from entry and how much time remained until expiration, I could be fortunate and suffer only a small loss or maybe even lock in a gain on the leg I am closing. Since the spread between the strikes I sold was pretty wide, I could hang onto the other position and not act unless and until the opposite trigger (support or resistance break) was hit.

Yet another possibility would be to close the whole trade only when an actual breakeven was hit. If little time remains until expiration, this choice would likely result in a relatively small loss, but if there was a great deal of time until expiration and volatility has increased, there is a chance that the loss could be more significant.

Suitability of Naked Straddles and Naked Strangles

As was the case with selling naked puts and selling naked calls, naked straddles and strangles are for traders who have time to monitor their positions and who are willing to take action promptly in accordance with a preconceived plan. Practice should definitely be undertaken before trading real money. While I agree that paper trading is not the same as trading with real money, it does help the trader to fully understand the nuances of the trades he is practicing. It helps achieve an understanding of how and when adjustments can and should be made without exposing the trader to losses resulting from ignorance and unpreparedness. It helps capture knowledge that is instrumental in creating the trade plan before the trade is entered.

The investor considering the inclusion of these strategies in his money machine will need first to have enough interest in this type of trade and then will need to understand the risks he will undertake. If those criteria are met, he should have the time and the desire to practice trade before putting real money at risk and must take the time to monitor the trade from entry to exit.

 GETTING INTO GEAR

In this chapter, we explored some option strategies that can provide a steady stream of income to the investor who is willing to take on the risks. We saw that selling naked puts can be a rewarding method to capture cash with no investment. It is a strategy best reserved for mildly bullish to very bullish situations. Selling naked calls, on the other hand is a device to generate income that should be reserved for bearish situations. Finally, naked straddles and strangles are designed to produce cash flow when volatility is relatively low and the security that forms the underlying is relatively stable.

Each of these tools can be quite effective in adding streams of income, but as we saw, they all have substantial risk. When selling out-of-the-money naked puts the trader will be successful if the stock price stays the same, goes up, or even if it goes down as long as it does not go below the strike price sold at expiration. Conversely, the sale of out-of-the-money naked calls will be successful if the stock price goes down, stays the same, or even if it goes up as long as it doesn't exceed the strike price sold at expiration. In the case of naked straddles and strangles, the investor will realize a gain as long as the stock price is between the breakevens at expiration. In the case of the naked straddle, the maximum return is achieved in the relatively rare situation where the stock price is exactly on the strike price at expiration while with the naked strangle, the maximum return is realized as long as the stock price is anywhere between the strike prices sold at expiration. Though the risk is high with these methods, the likelihood that any given trade will be profitable is also often quite high.

All these strategies do require relatively close monitoring. I don't mean that the investor has to have his nose pressed against the computer screen every day, but I do mean they are not suitable for a "set it and forget it" type of trade. Since the potential risks are so high the investor should have an adjustment and exit strategy in place before initiating the trade and must be willing to act when the signal for the adjustment or exit is hit.

These strategies are definitely not for the novice option trader, but can work quite well for the investor who is able and willing to make the effort to understand their workings and devote some time to practicing them.

CHAPTER 8

Bonds

Some Fasteners for the Machine

I remember my parents discussing a wealthy man they knew when I was a little boy. I asked them how come he was so rich and they said that all he did was sit around and clip coupons. I envisioned him sitting around with a pair of scissors and the newspaper carefully cutting discount coupons from the Acme Market meat ads. It occurred to me that seemed to be an easy way to make a lot of money and might be worth investigating. I learned, of course, that was not what my folks were referring to when they said the old fellow made his money clipping coupons.

Bonds historically have had coupons that originally were in the form of a piece of paper physically attached to the Bond Certificate that the investor would cut off and exchange for an interest payment. The coupons evidenced that the bearer was due a payment. Though almost all bonds today are issued electronically and have no physical coupon, the interest the issuer is obligated to pay may still be referred to as the coupon or the coupon rate.

Before I get too far ahead of myself, I should say that a bond is basically a promise to pay, or an IOU by which the borrower agrees to repay a lender with interest under specific conditions. Bonds come in a vast array of choices. They include obligations of federal, state, and local governments and authorities, big corporations, and even foreign governments. As the list would suggest, these are large borrowers who are borrowing very large amounts of money. Some are safer than others and some pay a higher coupon (interest rate on face value or par) than others. The date the principal is to be repaid varies from bond issue to bond issue and may be in a week or as long as 30 years. The interest on some is tax-free and the interest on others is taxable. In some cases the ability to repay may be based on the taxing power of the government; in others, it may be on a company's ability to generate income. Some bonds trade at a discount to their face value (par) and some at a premium to par.

While the many variations may seem to make the subject complex, as with many things, we can break them down element by element to reduce the complex to the simple and gain an understanding of how these securities can become a productive money machine part for us. In the next section, we'll begin to break down the parts of bonds we might want to consider before making a purchase, but, for now, suffice it to say that bonds can be "set it and forget it" income-producing investments or they can be devices with which we can be more active. In most cases they will be suitable for all three of our hypothetical investors, Forrest Footloose, the Middletons, and the Baldings since positions can be entered with relatively small amounts of capital and, if being used solely to produce interest income, with almost no monitoring at all.

THE ELEMENTS OF A BOND

As we examine bonds in general and any specific bond in particular, there are a number of factors we need to take into account. A number of these ingredients are common to all bonds and how they are combined can help us to decide whether to invest in any given issue. The list that follows discusses the basic elements of any bond and can be our starting point in any search for candidates in which to invest.

The Issuer. The issuer of a bond is the entity that is borrowing the money. Almost invariably the issuer is a large organization such as a government or a big corporation. Since large amounts of money are being borrowed, the issuer usually sells the bonds to a big underwriter like a Goldman Sachs or Merrill Lynch and they, in turn, sell the bonds to the investing public. Many times the bonds are purchased by large institutional investors like banks, pension funds, and insurance companies as well as by the "little guy," the retail investor. In exchange for the loan, the issuer legally obligates itself to the bondholder to do two things: (1) make periodic interest payments to the bondholder; and (2) return the principal to the bondholder at maturity.

The Indenture. The specific terms of the bond contract are set out in a legal document known as the indenture. Legalese aside, the indenture includes the total amount of the bond issue, the date the bond matures, the coupon rate, the frequency of interest payments, and whether and under what circumstances the bond is callable. Generally these are the specifics with which most investors would be concerned. In the following sections, we'll take a closer look at each of these obligations of the issuer as well as any right the issuer may have to call the bond.

Maturity. A bond is said to mature on the date the issuer is obligated to pay back the principal to the bondholder. The par value of a bond is its face value at the time of issue, quite often $1,000. Whatever that amount is, it is the amount the issuer is obligated to pay when the bond reaches maturity. The investor should understand that it is unlikely that the bond will trade at that exact price any time after issue until maturity. In other words the investor who bought five bonds each with a par value of $1,000 at the time of the original would have no assurance that he could sell the bond anytime before it matured for its face value. The value of the bond will fluctuate over time and may be worth more or less than $1,000 at any given moment until maturity, at which point it will be worth exactly $1,000 once again. Later in this chapter, we'll look at credit risk and interest rates and see how they influence bond pricing in conjunction with the coupon rate.

Coupon Rate. The coupon rate is the interest rate the issuer has agreed to pay. It is calculated on the par value of the bond so a $1,000 par value bond with a coupon rate of 6 percent is going to pay $60 a year in interest no matter at what price the bond may later be trading. If the bond is selling at a discount, the investor will still be paid $60, but if he bought the bond at $850 instead of at $1,000, his current yield would be 7 percent ($60 interest ÷ $850 cost). If the investor paid a premium and bought the bond at $1,500, his current yield would be only 4 percent ($60 interest ÷ $1,500 cost). The coupon rate, then, is a starting point to calculate what the actual current yield will be based on what we may pay for the bond.

Frequency of Interest Payments. Many bonds pay interest twice a year, while others may pay quarterly and others only annually. If an investor knows he will have certain financial obligations at specific times of year, he may consider buying bonds whose interest is paid at a time that is convenient to him in satisfying his obligations. We'll look at this concept toward the end of the chapter when we examine laddering as a method to create a bond portfolio. Some bonds, known as zero coupon bonds do not pay out any interest during the life of the bond, but include accumulated interest at maturity when redeemed. An investor might consider zero coupon bonds whose maturity coincides with some expected future event. New parents, for example, may choose to buy some zero coupon bonds that mature in 17 or 18 years to help fund a college education.

Call Provision. Some, though certainly not all, bonds have call provisions. That means that under certain circumstances that are defined in the indenture the issuer has the right to redeem, or call in, the bonds and repay the bondholders before the maturity date. This provision is a protection for the issuer who may find that sometime after issue he may be able to borrow money for less than the coupon rate. If that circumstance arises, the issuer would like to have the ability, in effect, to refinance the debt by repaying the bondholders and perhaps borrow the money elsewhere at a lower rate or float a new bond issue at a lower coupon rate. When a bond is called, the bondholder is repaid par or, depending on the terms of the Indenture, perhaps par plus a little.

Having a bond called before maturity ordinarily is not a benefit to the bondholder. The issuer is only going to call the bonds when it is to its advantage and that would mean that interest rates are lower. If interest rates have dropped, it is likely that the bond may be trading at a premium to par so when called the bondholder will lose any premium over par as a potential capital gain and since current interest rates are lower than the coupon, it is unlikely that the investor could get as good a rate as he had enjoyed with the bond that was called. In other words, he will not be able to enjoy the same rate that otherwise would have been locked-in until maturity.

PRICING ISSUES

Like all markets, bond markets are always in motion so the price of bonds will change over time. Several factors influence the price of bonds. Two, in particular, exert great influence on pricing: interest rates and credit risk (or rating). Movement in either or both of these categories will result in movement of bond prices and current yield for the buyer. We'll examine these along with the importance of callability in the following sections. As we look at these risks, we should be cognizant of the phenomenon that we can expect price swings resulting from the risks to be greater the longer the length of time to maturity.

Interest Rates

As we saw, the coupon rate is the rate of interest paid on the par value of the bond. If we have a $1,000 bond with a coupon rate of 8 percent, it is going to pay $80 a year and if the coupon rate is 5 percent it is going to pay $50 a year no matter at what price the bond may be trading. If we buy a $1,000 bond at par, we pay $1,000. If it has a coupon rate of 8 percent, it will pay $80 a year in interest until maturity unless the issuer defaults. Suppose that after we bought the bond for $1,000, interest rates dropped for several months until they landed at 5 percent. Our bond is paying 8 percent but investors can only get 5 percent now. Is our bond worth more or less than the $1,000 we paid? It's probably worth more. To get the same $80 a year at 5 percent, the investor would have to invest about $1,600 ($1,600 × 5 percent = $80) so now our bond should be worth closer to $1,600 than the $1,000 we paid in the first place. What if interest rates got higher? Suppose that they went to 12 percent. Now our bond would probably be worth less than the $1,000 we paid. In order to get the same $80 a year at a current 12 percent rate, the investor would only have to invest about $667 ($667 × 12 percent = $80) so our bond would only be worth about $667. That isn't a good situation if we needed to sell the bond at that point. However, if we had no need for the cash, we could just keep our bond until maturity when we would get our $1,000 back.

We've already seen that different bonds have different maturities and the time to maturity is an important factor in interest rate risk. The further out the maturity, in general, the higher the interest rate risk. If we buy a noncallable bond just to lock-in a long-term interest rate we may not care about fluctuations in the market price because we intend to hold it to maturity anyway at which time we expect we will be repaid the par value. That investment when we know we are holding to maturity and have no reason to believe we may need the principal in the interim is a "set it and forget it." However, if we might have a need for the principal before maturity, we definitely must be aware of the risk associated with interest rate change. Even if the bond is insured or is a U.S. government issue, it does not mean that we can get par or the face value at any time. The guarantee only guarantees timely interest payments and redemption at par at maturity.

All bonds are subject to interest rate risk. Since we know that bonds will move in response to interest rate movement, we just need to keep in mind that the price of a bond is likely to go up when interest rates drop and the price of a bond is likely to go down when interest rates rise.

Credit Risk

Another important component that affects the price of a bond is the creditworthiness of the issuer and the relative potential risk of default. Since there are so many bonds and so many issuers, it would take a herculean effort to make these assessments by any individual investor. Fortunately, there are credit-rating agencies that do the work for us. The three well-known credit-reporting agencies are Standard & Poor's, Moody's, and Fitch. These organizations perform a financial analysis to attempt to determine the financial health of the issuer as well as its ability to make timely interest payments and to repay the loan at maturity. Once the analysis has been completed, they assign a rating that can help the investor decide what action, if any, he may take.

Before exploring the rating systems, we should be aware that any security that is issued directly by the United States government is to have no risk of default. Since they are deemed to have no risk of default, U.S. government securities such as savings bonds and Treasuries are not rated. Those securities are considered to be of the highest quality and the most secure.

Other bonds, including those issued by municipalities and corporations, are rated by the agencies. Each of the agencies uses a lettering system to rate credit quality. Though the alphabet soup differs slightly among the agencies, the highest rating (perceived lowest risk) is AAA for Standard & Poor's and Fitch and is denominated Aaa for Moody's. BBB is the lowest investment grade for Standard & Poor's and Baa the lowest investment grade for Moody's. Anything below that rating (e.g., BB or B for S&P or Ba or B for Moody's) is considered junk and high risk. When a bond is rated as investment grade the rating agency has concluded that there is a relatively low risk of default either in interest payments or in redemption at maturity.

The investor does need to be aware that these ratings can change over the life of the bond. An issuer that was strong and solvent at the time of the initial rating could fall on hard times and its ability to satisfy its obligations become less certain. In circumstances such as that, the credit-rating agencies might lower the rating. If the original rating was AAA and the rating dropped to AA, it may affect the bond price, but in terms of the likelihood of default, the rating change probably means little since both categories are still indicators of high quality. However, if the rating should drop from BBB to B by Standard & Poor's or from B to Caa by Moody's, the change would be significant since the bond would no longer be considered to be investment grade; it would now have fallen to the status of "junk" with higher risk.

Whenever there is higher risk, the investor expects a higher reward so credit rating becomes quite important in the price of bonds. If, for example, an issuer has poor credit and a bond receives a low rating (e.g., S&P or Moody's C), it will undoubtedly have to pay a higher coupon rate at issue than an issuer whose bond has a AAA or Aaa rating. No smart investor would want to take on a higher risk for the same return so if the coupon rates were the same, at the time of issue the AAA-rated bond would naturally be chosen over the C-rated security.

Some bonds are insured. In general, this attribute is most likely found in municipal bonds and when insured, the bonds will have a higher credit rating than those that are uninsured. In exchange for the higher credit rating, we can expect a slightly lower coupon rating. It is important to understand exactly what is insured. Market price is not insured so we can't expect to sell our $1,000 par value for $1,000 on the open market if it happens to be trading at $700. The insurance guarantees timely payment of interest and repayment at maturity, nothing else. Even with insurance, the investor still needs to exercise caution because the insurance is only as good as the insurer's ability to pay and, following the revelations about the credit crisis in the mid- to latter 2000s, that isn't as clear as it once was. The insurance does afford some level of protection but historically there have been relatively few defaults on municipal bonds anyway.

Credit risk plays an important role in the price of a bond. At the time of issue, bonds that have a lower credit rating will have a higher coupon rate. Once marketed, the price of a bond will go up if the rating goes higher and the price will drop if the rating is lowered. The change in price does a great deal to reflect current yield. If we started by buying a BBB-rated bond at par value of $1,000 at issue with a coupon rate of 7.5 percent when the interest rate (as determined by the long Treasury) was 5 percent and the rating on our bond later dropped to C, what would happen? Naturally, the price of our bond would drop so that the current yield would be in line with other similarly rated bonds with similar maturity. If the current yield on C-rated bonds with a similar maturity was then 11 percent, our $1,000 par value bond with a 7.5 percent coupon would only be worth about $680. At maturity we would still get back the $1,000, but at the moment if we had to sell it we would only get about $680. The reason is that bonds with similar credit risk and maturity are commanding a current yield of 11 percent and our bond is only paying a coupon of 7.5 percent. That means our bond is paying $75 a year in interest no matter where it is priced. A bond buyer would only pay enough so that an 11 percent return on his purchase price would bring in $75 a year in interest. Whether he bought the bond for $1,000 or $500 or $800, he would still get $75 a year in interest, no more, no less. So the investor needs to find out on what amount 11 percent interest will yield $75. To calculate that amount, all we need to do is divide $75 by 11 percent to see that we should not pay more than $681.82 if we want to lock in the 11 percent.

Call Risk

In some cases, the issuer retains a right to call in or buy the bond before the maturity date. The existence of that right can be detrimental to the bondholder. Suppose we bought a 10-year $1,000 par value bond at issue with an 8.5 percent coupon rate that now has seven years left until maturity. We initially bought the bond to lock in an interest rate we liked at the time. The bond has a provision that permits the issuer to call the bond at par three years from issue, which is where we are now. Meanwhile, interest rates have dropped to 5 percent. Now, but for the call provision, our bond would be worth about $1,700 since it generates $85 a year and in order to get $85 a year at 5 percent (current rates), we would need to invest $1,700 ($1,700 \times 5$ percent $= \$85$). From the issuer's viewpoint it could retire the debt on which it is paying 8.5 percent interest and refinance the debt for around 5 percent so it quite likely will call the bond at par. Under those circumstances, at least you'll get your $1,000 back, but you wouldn't be able to get the extra $700 capital gain and you will no longer be getting 8.5 percent on your money. If you reinvest the $1,000 for a similar maturity and a bond of approximately equal rating, you will probably only be able to get an interest rate around 5 percent so you'll be missing out on 3.5 percent interest along with the potential capital gain. If you bought the bond at a premium instead of at par and the bond is called, you will lose some or all of the premium since the bond will be redeemed at par (or, in some cases, slightly above par).

We can see that the call risk can be fairly dramatic if interest rates fall so if we are considering a bond that has call provisions we would either expect to get a higher coupon rate or pay less than for a similar rated bond with the same maturity.

Trading Risks

Though there is an active bond trading market, it is a much different game than trading stocks. Several issues present themselves when trading bonds. Just getting pricing information can be a difficult proposition though with the advent of the Internet it is becoming somewhat easier. Some online brokers, for example, now quote bonds that are available for sale. However, if you already own a bond that you want to sell, it may be hard to find a bid and it is probably wise to seek bids from a number of brokers. Commissions are built into spreads so it is difficult at times to find what the bond price is and what the commission is. Often the spreads between what a buyer will pay and what a seller is asking are quite wide. So if a trader bought a bond and found he needed to or wanted to sell it, he could be faced with a fairly large loss just on the spread alone. When trading a bond, the investor should not hesitate to try to negotiate with the broker to sell somewhat higher than the bid or to buy somewhat below the offer. In addition to whatever hidden markup or markups may be in the pricing, the broker also may (often does) charge a transaction fee.

Inflation Risk

As they say, everything is relative. We might buy a bond with a current yield of 8 percent and be very happy. Unless called, we have locked-in a 7 percent interest rate until maturity. In terms of buying power, that could be good or bad. Suppose inflation is running at a 3 percent rate. Our real rate of return then would be 4 percent, which is generally considered to be good. To look at it one way, 3 percent of our interest keeps us even with inflation and the other 4 percent puts us ahead; in a sense we are gaining ground. What if a couple of years go by and inflation suddenly jumps to 9 percent? Now, we would be losing ground. Speaking simplistically, we are losing ground since the interest we earn is not keeping up with the inflation. That is a risk we always run when we own longer-term debt securities with fixed interest rates.

I often wonder about the wisdom of savings accounts in that regard. Often, savings accounts pay a low interest rate, lower than inflation so the saver is putting his money in a position where it is guaranteed to lose buying power as long as the interest rate doesn't at least equal the inflation rate. In one of the sections on government obligations that follow, we'll see something known as a TIPS, which is designed to protect against the risks of inflation.

TYPES OF BONDS

We've just seen the basic elements of a bond and explored some of the risks of bond ownership. In the sections that follow, we'll take a look at many of the various types of bonds that are available and how they might be used to accomplish individual investor goals. In general, we can expect a trade-off between the relative risk to which we are exposing ourselves and the interest rate we will be paid. Naturally, the lower the risk, the lower the interest rate. We'll start by looking at some securities issued directly by the United States government that are considered to have no risk of default. Please note that I said no risk *of default*. There may be market risk during the life of the bond so we need to be careful not to confuse the two.

U.S. Government Securities

Most of our emphasis throughout the book has been on strategies that produce current streams of income. While that approach will continue, there are times when we can set up an investment to mature at a specific time to satisfy some specific circumstance, such as a child going to college or retirement. As we investigate U.S. government bonds, it is a good time to differentiate between the so-called coupon bonds and accrual bonds. Coupon bonds pay interest regularly; in the case of U.S. government bonds, usually twice a year. Accrual bonds, on the other hand, are earning interest but do not pay it out until the bonds are redeemed. Depending on the bond, taxes may be due on the interest as it accrues each year even though it is not actually paid to the bondholder, and in other cases the payment of taxes on interest may be deferred or, in certain circumstances, eliminated if the proceeds are used to fund for designated higher education. We'll identify the coupon type and accrual types in sections that follow about the safest of all investments—direct obligations of the United States.

Savings Bonds   Savings Bonds are probably the government bonds with which most people are familiar. Currently the government is issuing two types of Savings Bonds, the EE/E and the I, which are of the accrual type. There are a number of similarities between the two and a couple of significant differences. I Bonds and EE Bonds have the following six characteristics in common:

1. Interest earnings are exempt from state and local income taxes (though they are subject to state and local excise, gift, or inheritance taxes).
2. They can be in any denomination of $25 or more.
3. There is a purchase limit of $5,000 per year per Social Security number.
4. Either can be redeemed after a year, but if redeemed between one and five years there is a penalty of the most recent three months of interest.
5. Both the I and the EE Bonds can be purchased electronically through TreasuryDirect, through payroll savings, or through most financial institutions.
6. Interest earnings may be excluded from federal income tax when used for higher education (we'll review those circumstances shortly).

The most significant difference between the EE Bonds (purchased after May, 2005) and the I Bonds is that the EE Bonds return a fixed rate of interest while the I Bonds have an interest rate comprised of a fixed rate plus a semiannually adjusted inflation rate. In other words, the I Bond builds in an inflation protection that the EE Bond does not.

In the case of I Bonds, the inflation rate portion of the interest is reset every six months based upon the CPI-U (Consumer Price Index - Urban). As inflation rises, the inflation indexed variable part of the rate increases and as inflation drops, so, too, would that element of the interest. The other element of the interest calculation, the fixed rate, remains the same. Since they are not traded in secondary markets and can be redeemed after a year, there is no risk that the value of the bonds will go down before maturity as would exist with other types of bonds whose value will fluctuate between issue and maturity. In addition, they earn tax-deferred interest on interest until redeemed. All I Bonds are sold at face value whether purchased as paper bonds or electronically. Things are a little different for the EE Bonds.

EE Bonds have a fixed maturity so there is no built-in inflation protection though they could be redeemed after a year if inflation increased and new bonds at presumably higher interest rates could be purchased. At a minimum, EE bonds are guaranteed to double in value by 20 years from the date they are issued. There is a difference in price between buying the EE's electronically and as paper bonds. When bought electronically, they are sold at face value; that is we pay $100 for a $100 bond or $25 for a $25 bond. However, if we buy paper EE bonds we pay half the face value or $50 for a $100 bond. There is no advantage since the paper bonds are not worth the face value until maturity while the electronic bonds are worth full value when available for redemption.

Even though interest accrues with these bonds rather than pays out regularly, they can be valuable assets for specific purposes, particularly events that we know will be five years or longer away. In the interim, if we do need the money we can redeem the bonds at any time after a year and get back our principal with accrued interest (except we are penalized three months' most recent interest). After five years, these bonds can be redeemed at any time without penalty and with accrued interest. They can be particularly valuable as investments to pay for higher education.

Education Tax Exclusion   Before investigating the current tax benefits of these EE and I Bonds if used to fund education, I want to add the caveat that I am anything but a tax expert and I urge you to consult a tax specialist before acting on the tax information set out here (and, for that matter, anywhere in this book). It is also important to recognize that the tax code changes fairly often, depending on the politics of the time so anything you see here may change between the time I write it and the time you read it or may want to act upon it.

In any event, for the time being, at least, what is known as the education tax exclusion permits certain taxpayers to exclude all or part of the interest paid at redemption of EE or I Bonds from gross income if the bond owner pays enumerated higher education expenses at an eligible institution. The following are requirements that must be met in order to exclude the interest from gross income for federal tax purposes[*]:

- Qualified higher education expenses must be incurred in the same tax year in which the bonds are redeemed.
- Qualified expenses are those paid for tuition and fees (not books or room or board) or for any course required for a degree or certificate granting program and must be paid for yourself, your spouse, or dependent claimed as an exemption on your tax return.
- When using bonds for a child's education, the bond must be registered in your name or your spouse's name and the child cannot be listed as a co-owner on the bond.
- When using bonds for your own education, they must be registered in your own name.
- If married, you must file a joint return.
- You must meet certain income requirements; that is income must be beneath a specified level (for example, in 2006 the exclusion was limited to couples with adjusted gross income below $124,700) and that amount can be expected to change from time to time.
- Both principal and interest must be used to pay the educational expenses.
- The educational institution must be a college, university, or vocational school that meets the standards for federal assistance.
- You have to be at least 24 years old by the first day of the month on which you bought the bonds.

As you can see, there are quite a few hoops through which to jump, but none is particularly difficult as long as you know they are there in the first place. Again, be sure you check the current requirements if you are considering an investment in these bonds for educational purposes and again at the time right before you redeem them to see if any criteria have been added, changed, or removed. It seems most likely that the maximum income ceiling is one of the most likely qualifications we would expect to change over time so that is certainly something to check before redeeming and using the funds for higher education expenses.

---

[*]IRS Publication 17, "Your Federal Income Tax" and IRS Publication 550, "Investment Income and Expenses." Note that the rules set out above were current as of the time of this writing, but, as with all things political, could change in the future. Always check with your tax professional for up-to-date requirements.

Treasury Notes   Treasury Notes or T-Notes are fixed interest obligations issued with maturities of 2, 5, and 10 years. They are sold in increments of $100. These Notes are now only issued and held electronically. There no longer are any paper T-Notes. They pay coupon interest at the fixed rate semi-annually. As with other Treasury obligations, T-Notes are not callable and are redeemable at face value at maturity.

Between issue and maturity, there is a liquid market for treasuries. They can be traded easily and have neither credit risk nor call risk though they do have interest rate risk. For that reason, when interest rates rise, the market value of the T-Note will decline and the T-Note could be bought at a discount and, conversely, when interest rates fall, the bonds increase in market value at which time they may command a premium. Smaller price changes are expected with shorter maturities and greater changes would occur with longer maturities. Of course, at maturity, the bondholder is paid face value.

The interest on T-Notes is free of state or local income taxes though federal income taxes must be paid on interest and on capital gains, if any. They can be purchased through TreasuryDirect, brokers, banks, or dealers.

Treasury Notes are safe investments that provide a known flow of interest payments twice a year at the rate fixed at auction. Principal will be repaid at maturity, but unless the investor intends to hold until maturity, he conceivably could suffer a loss of principal if he had to sell the Note at a discount after an increase in rates.

Treasury Bonds   Treasury Bonds bear regular fixed rate coupon interest and are similar to Treasury Notes except that they have a longer term until maturity; that is, 30 years. Since the term is longer, T-Bonds can generally be expected to have a higher fixed interest rate than T-Notes issued around the same time, but they also carry a higher risk from changes in interest rates since there is so much more time to maturity. Larger discounts and larger premiums for T-Bonds can be expected with movements in interest rates.

Treasury Bonds are also sold in increments of $100 and are now issued only in electronic form although there are still some around in paper form. Those bonds in paper form can be converted to electronic form easily if the owner chooses. Interest is taxable by the federal government but is exempt from state and local income taxes.

As with the Treasury Notes, the fixed rate is determined at auction and once issued, the Treasury Bonds can be traded through TreasuryDirect, banks, brokers, or dealers. Since these bonds are so actively traded, the investor can find and purchase almost any maturity he might desire, which can be helpful in using a laddering approach as we'll see toward the end of the chapter when we examine some bond-trading strategies.

Risk to the investor in T-Bonds lies in interest rate movement and can be significant if the bonds are not held until maturity. A sharp rise in interest rates while a bond has a lot of time until maturity can result in a dramatic discount from par and could result in a loss of principal if the investor has to sell the bond. The opposite is true as well, and the owner could enjoy a gain if the bond trades at a premium to par following a drop in rates.

Unless the investor intends to try to trade on interest rate movement, my suggestion is that the Treasury Bonds might best be treated as buy-and-hold investments where the owner creates a stream of income from coupon interest at a level acceptable to him.

Treasury Bills   At the opposite end of the maturity spectrum from Treasury Bonds lie the T-Bills or Treasury Bills. These are obligations of the accrual type where the investor buys at a discount and redeems at face value and the difference between the discounted price paid and the face value is the interest. T-Bills are sold in increments of $100 and are offered in maturities of 4, 13, 26, and 52 weeks. All but the 52-week maturities are auctioned each week and the 52-week bills are auctioned every four weeks. As with the Treasury Bonds and Treasury Notes, the interest on the T-Bills is exempt from state and local taxes, but is subject to federal income tax. They can be purchased from the same sources as we have already mentioned and they can be sold at or before maturity.

TIPS   Depending on conditions, TIPS, the acronym for Treasury Inflation-Protected Securities, can be attractive investments. TIPS are available in increments of $100 and in terms of 5, 10, and 20 years. The interest rate is set at the time of auction and remains fixed. However, the principal value of a TIPS moves with inflation as measured by the CPI-U. As inflation increases, the principal value of the TIPS grows and as inflation decreases, the principal value declines although it never goes below the original principal. Since the value of principal moves with inflation, so, too, does the amount of the interest payments. Although the interest rate remains fixed, the amount paid would be larger if paid on a higher principal and smaller if paid on a lower principal amount.

Interest payments are made twice a year and they are exempt from state and local taxes though subject to federal income tax as are any gains in principal, which are taxed as capital gains. Taxes are assessed on the interest and on any gains in principal in the taxable year in which they occur so a TIPS holder will be obligated to pay taxes on those items even when no payment has actually been received. Reductions in principal from deflation will show as losses for the taxable year in which they might occur.

TIPS are held only in electronic form. Just as with the other government obligations we have reviewed, TIPS can be bought and sold through the same TreasuryDirect, banks, brokers, or dealers. Since they are marketable, they can be held until maturity or sold before maturity in the secondary market. They are subject to interest and, perhaps, issues of liquidity, but if held to maturity should assure a real rate of return that is greater than inflation.

You may have noted that TIPS are similar to I Bonds, but there are some very important differences. I Bonds are not marketable and do not trade in secondary markets so there is no risk that their value will go down in response to increasing interest rates as could be the case with TIPS. TIPS are marketable, but the market price can vary with interest rates and liquidity. Inflation adjustments to TIPS are made monthly while I Bond adjustments are made semiannually. As we just noted, the interest and inflation adjustments on TIPS are taxable in the year they occur while the reporting of interest on I Bonds may be deferred until maturity or redemption. I Bonds pay interest based on two factors, the fixed rate of return at purchase and the variable inflation rate while TIPS pay a fixed rate of interest, but based on a principal amount that fluctuates with inflation.

If the investor does not need current income and expects to hold until maturity, a TIPS can provide a secure way to assure a return greater than inflation over the life of the security with no risk to principal.

Zero Coupons Though certainly not unique to government securities, zero coupon bonds are often backed with Treasuries so now is as good a time as any to describe them and check out some of the pros and cons. Zero coupon bonds do not pay out interest during the life of the bonds. Though their term to maturity is much longer, they, like T-Bills are purchased at a discount to their face value. Since there is a long time to maturity (10 years or more in many cases) the discount is usually quite deep. At maturity, the owner is paid face value, and the difference between the deeply discounted purchase price and the face value is the imputed interest.

The only zero coupons the U.S. Treasury actually issues itself are the T-Bills. It does have a program called the STRIPS program that enables the disaggregation of coupon and principal payments of Treasury notes, bonds, or TIPS so that they can be stripped and separately traded as zero coupons.

As we discussed with interest on TIPS, tax is levied on the phantom interest each year even though it is not actually received at that time by the bondholder. As a result, an investor might consider holding these in some tax-sheltered account like an IRA, or possibly in a child's account where earnings would not be expected to be high.

Some positive features of zeros are that we know exactly what the return will be and when the face value will be available. We can buy them with a maturity that coincides with our expected needs. They also can be traded in secondary markets and that can be either good or bad.

The market price of zero coupon bonds can be very volatile and can be expected to have greater price swings than coupon bonds since they pay no interest. When interest rates go up, there can be sharp declines in the price of the bond and that isn't good if circumstances require you to sell it. On the other hand, if interest rates fall, the value of the bond can increase fairly dramatically and that can be a good thing if you bought the bond to trade rather than to hold until maturity.

As a general rule and since I don't consider myself to be an active bond trader, the taxable zero coupons would only interest me when yields were particularly attractive. I should mention that there are zero coupon municipals that may be of interest since the phantom interest is not taxable. We'll look at municipals in general a couple of sections later in this chapter. Otherwise, the taxable zero coupons would seem to work better in the tax-sheltered accounts.

TreasuryDirect   The United States Treasury has a very convenient web site that enables individual investors to open an account and purchase the various Treasury securities we have examined in the preceding sections. TreasuryDirect® can be accessed at treasurydirect.gov and once an account is opened the investor can access it 24/7 to buy, sell, hold, and manage T-Bills, T-Bonds, T-Notes, Savings Bonds, and TIPS all online. There is no charge and there are no fees to buy or maintain securities in a TreasuryDirect account. There is a modest fee ($45 at the time of this writing) to sell marketable securities in the secondary markets through the SellDirect feature. When selling, the requests are transmitted to the Federal Reserve Bank of Chicago where the securities are sold to the highest bidding securities broker.

As you have seen, marketable Treasuries can also be bought and sold through banks, dealers, and brokers. I would suggest checking out the comparative charges of these intermediaries and comparing them to TreasuryDirect since it may be possible to enjoy substantial savings, particularly on a percentage basis when making a number of small investments.

Municipal Bonds

Many investors have at least a nodding familiarity with municipal bonds (sometimes called munis) since most offer interest that is free of federal income tax, and in some cases, free of state income tax as well. Just as the Treasuries we covered in the earlier sections are the obligation of the

United States government, municipal bonds are the obligations of states, counties, cities, and municipal authorities. In some cases they are issued by entities like hospitals or universities or other authorities that have some public purpose.

One very important distinction between munis and Treasuries is that the Treasuries are considered to be completely safe and have no credit risk while municipal bonds are rated by the credit-rating agencies. In addition to interest rate risks as discussed in previous sections, municipal bonds also have credit risk and may have a call risk as well. An important factor in assessing credit risk is whether the bond is a general obligation of the issuing political subdivision or whether it will be repaid from revenues as might be the case with a parking authority or perhaps a hospital bond.

General Obligation Bonds have the backing of the taxing power of the entity so may be considered to have a lower risk than a Revenue Bond that primarily is dependent on the earnings of a project. In any event, the General Obligation Bonds tend to pay a somewhat lower coupon rate than Revenue Bonds, but the investor should keep in mind that many Revenue Bonds may also have high credit ratings as well. One other factor that can affect a bond's rating is whether it is insured. Insurance at least adds a layer of protection and adds some strength to the rating of a given bond. I emphasize that it is a layer of protection only since the insurance companies themselves could run into trouble from any serious credit crisis. In any event, the risk of default is diminished by some degree from the very existence of the insurance (assuming a solvent insurance company). The coupon rate on the insured bonds will generally be a little lower than it might otherwise have been since the issuer's credit rating alone would have provided less security than the issuer's rating plus insurance.

Undoubtedly one of the lures of municipal bonds is that they are federally tax-free. Since they are tax-free, municipal bonds tend to pay a lower rate than bonds with similar credit ratings and maturities that are taxable. The investor should be aware that just because interest on a muni is not taxable does not necessarily mean it will give him the best after-tax return. Because of the relatively heavy demand for tax-frees, the prices in the secondary market may be somewhat inflated leading to lower yields. As a result, the investor may find better after-tax yields with similarly rated corporate bonds. For that reason, the smart investor will always compare after-tax yields of other taxable issues of similarly rated bonds with similar maturities to the yields of municipals he might be investigating. A simple formula can be used to determine what taxable equivalent yield is equal to the tax-exempt yield. The formula is:

Taxable equivalent yield = tax − exempt yield ÷ (1 − tax bracket)

If an investor is in the 28 percent tax bracket and is looking at a muni with a 5 percent tax-exempt yield he could see that a taxable yield of 6.94 percent (taxable yield = 5 ÷ (1 − .28) or taxable yield = 5 ÷ .72 = 6.94) would net him the same after-tax income. As long as the taxable bond has a yield higher than 6.94 percent, the investor is better off buying the taxable bond. In the example, if the investor could find a corporate bond with a similar rating and a similar maturity yielding 7.5 percent he would be better off from an income standpoint (net after taxes) to buy the corporate bond.

I should mention that not all municipal bonds are tax-free. In this day of communities buying sports stadiums for their teams, the financing may well come from a bond issue. These situations arise when the bonds are issued for private purposes like a baseball or football team rather than something that would be deemed to be essential for the public good.

Municipals are also sometimes issued as zero coupon bonds. They are almost universally subject to call, but the call price is set at some specific discount to the par value. Since there is a long time to maturity, these issues also can be quite volatile. Credit ratings become extremely important since the issuer has to pay out no interest until maturity. An investor would certainly be wise to undertake a little investigation to determine how strong the issuer is and is likely to be over time until maturity. If the issuer is a community that has lost its major or only industry and population is rapidly dwindling, I would think twice before buying their zero coupon bond with 15 years to maturity.

As with many bonds, markups and commissions are difficult to ascertain with anything close to precision. In addition, that problem can be aggravated because many bonds are bought in relatively small lots, which can be a hassle for a dealer and leads only to higher costs, particularly if the investor is a seller. For these reasons, the municipal bond may best be used as an income source for a buy-and-hold position until maturity.

An alternative to buying individual municipal bonds may be to purchase a closed-end municipal bond fund where the ability to trade in and out is much less troublesome. In exchange for the greatly enhanced liquidity, the shareholder is charged a small management and/or administrative fee. At the same time, the fund holds a variety of bonds so risk of an individual default is significantly reduced.

Corporate Bonds

Corporate bonds are the obligations of companies to repay money they borrow from bondholders. Though they will have a higher coupon rate than treasuries or munis, the risk may be higher and the interest on corporate bonds is taxable at all levels. Investors can find bonds in various sectors of the economy including financials, transportation, utilities, and industrial.

As is the case with municipals, corporate bonds are rated by the various rating agencies, but corporate bonds are rated by issue rather than by the issuer as is the case with municipals. It is important with corporate bonds to have individual issues rated because corporations may issue several series of bonds and the more senior bonds will have priority of payment over the junior bonds in the event things go awry.

Credit ratings are very important for corporates and credit risk is difficult to assess because so many variables come into play. Even once assessed, the ratings can change frequently as elements like the economy, prospects for the industry, product or services development, or even management change.

Corporate bonds are subject to interest risk and call risk as well. Many corporates have call provisions that can be exercised under a number of circumstances. The provisions will be unique to the bond, but may be permitted in some cases simply if the issuer is able to find a cheaper source of capital. In any event, a prospective buyer should familiarize himself with the call criteria specific to his bond. Interest risk is similar to what we have examined in the preceding sections. With risks higher than Treasuries and, in many cases, higher than municipals, the companies issuing bonds needs to make them attractive to investors so they sometimes provide added enticements.

Some Optional Accessories   Agile minds have created many perks attached to corporate bonds to make them attractive to investors over the years. Put bonds and floating rates are a couple of examples.

In order to alleviate some of the credit risk, bonds may have what are known as put features. Put bonds allow the bondholder to put (resell) the bond to the issuer before maturity at par. The bondholder of a put bond can avoid at least some of the interest rate risk when rates rise by exercising the put and selling the bond back to the issuer then reinvesting the money at the new higher rate in some other security.

Another device to make some corporate bonds more attractive is a floating rate feature. These bonds periodically adjust the interest rate based on some benchmark so that the bondholder has some protection against rising rates. In some cases the bond may have a floor below which the interest rate cannot go.

Other features may make a given bond more attractive to investors. Some corporate bonds, known as convertibles, may be exchanged for stock under defined circumstances. Other bonds may come with warrants that entitle the bondholder to buy shares of stock at a specific price in the future. The warrants are similar to call options where the owner has the right, but not the obligation, to buy the stock at a certain price within a certain time.

Treasure in the Junk Pile   Bonds that are rated as noninvestment grade are known as junk bonds. Since junk bonds are rated below investment quality there is a higher risk of default and the issuer has to do something to make them attractive enough that they will be bought. The answer is high to very high yields and maturities generally in the 5- to 10-year range. Credit risk is high enough without adding a very long maturity to add to the mix.

By definition, there is a relatively high risk of default with junk bonds so the investor might want to diversify among the junk and have several issues to spread the risk or, perhaps, consider buying shares in a closed-end high-yield bond fund that has at least part of its portfolio in junk. By using the closed-end fund, the trader can enjoy the benefits of relatively high yield combined with decent liquidity and the ability to trade in and out of the position with relative ease. Owning the individual bonds, in addition to high risk, will likely present a liquidity problem and result in difficulty if the bondholder attempts to sell before maturity.

Junk bonds are for the true speculator or someone willing to accept a high risk in exchange for a high yield.

International Bonds

International bonds, as you have guessed, are bonds of foreign governments or foreign companies. They add layers of risks to credit and interest risk they share with the various classes of domestic bonds we have reviewed. Currency risk becomes an important factor with these bonds and, of course, as with anything in the future currency exchange is not predictable. The currency risk can exist both at the time the bonds are purchased and at the time they are sold or redeemed. With many international bonds, U.S. dollars must be converted into the foreign currency when the bonds are purchased and the foreign currency must be converted back into dollars when the bond is sold or redeemed. Added to that is the issue not only whether the foreign entity is able to redeem the bonds, but also whether it is willing to fulfill its obligation. In most cases, if able, the issuer would probably be willing to repay since it might want to issue other bonds in the future. However, there certainly could be exceptions with changing foreign relations.

If we think that analyzing a domestic corporation has a lot of variables, imagine how many issues exist in trying to analyze a foreign government or a foreign corporation. The task is difficult and complex and exposes the investor to a great deal of risk. Though returns may sometimes be quite good, these are generally highly speculative investments.

In my estimation, it would be the rare investor who should consider placing individual issues of international bonds in his portfolio. If an investor is considering an investment because he likes the return on bonds from emerging nations like China or India he may seek an ETF (Exchange Traded Fund) or closed-end international bond fund that includes emerging nations in its holdings. Some ETFs include international bonds in their holdings. iShares JP Morgan USD Emerging Markets Bond Fund ETF (EMB), for example, attempts to track the JPMorgan EMBI Global Core Index price and yield performance in U.S. dollars.

I mention that ETF only to provide an example of a security that may be available to invest in a diverse position in the international bond market. The ETFs have important advantages over buying individual issues in the foreign markets. They are liquid and easily traded enabling the investor to get in and out essentially at will and since they represent a basket of bonds they do not have the same risk as an individual issue might have.

International bonds are for the aggressive investor who is willing to undertake a relatively large risk in exchange for a potentially significant reward. My suggestion is to avoid these bonds unless you consider yourself to be a high roller and use only pure risk money; money that won't hurt you to lose. If you are in that situation, you may find some good yields at various times.

STRATEGIES FOR BOND INVESTING

There are a number of ways to approach bond investing and as we have seen with other investments covered in the book much of what an investor might do is dependent on age and what is happening in their lives. Before we return to Forrest Footloose, the Middletons, and the Baldings, there are a couple of general concepts of bond investing that may be helpful.

Laddering

Laddering in its most elementary form simply means buying bonds with different maturities. It is a buy-and-hold strategy that helps smooth interest rate risks. The investor might begin by buying bonds with maturities of 3, 5, 7, and 10 years for example. The closer maturity bonds would have a lesser yield while the longer maturities would have a higher yield. Assuming they are coupon bonds, the investor would get income twice a year from each bond and when each hit maturity, he could reinvest the principal at the far end of the ladder. Adding complexity to suit an individual's situation is also possible. The investor might decide he wants income in April, July, October, and January, in which case he could buy the maturities he wanted plus find bonds that made their interest payments in those months.

Finding those would require more work, but, if found, would satisfy the specific needs.

Zero coupons could also be laddered so that payments of interest and principal would be received at known times in the future. An investor with a young child might prepare for college by buying zeros that mature during the years when the child reaches college age and the three or four years following. In that way, a parent could use present dollars to create a fund or series of funds payable at predetermined times in the future. Folks could ladder bonds to mature at set times during retirement or for whatever other reason they might choose.

Barbells

The barbell strategy is one where the investor owns bonds with long maturities and bonds with short maturities, but none with intermediate maturities. The 20- or 30-year bonds could be expected to provide decent coupon rates while providing a lower coupon rate, the bonds with a two-year or shorter maturity will make capital available to reinvest in more short terms or some other investment if the bond market turns down.

From a speculative perspective, an investor might consider buying long maturities when he believes rates may decline. If he is right, his bonds will have a higher market value and, consequently, an added capital gain. Holding shorter maturities can help if the guess is wrong and rates stay the same or increase.

One scenario that endangers the effectiveness of the strategy is if long-term rates rise and short-term rates fall. In that situation, the market value of the long maturities would dip, as would the yield on the short maturities.

EXAMPLES

Using the same characters as we have throughout this book, we'll look at ways investors at various ages and with varying needs might structure bond investments.

Forrest Footloose: TIPS in an IRA or a Bond Fund

Our hypothetical young single or newly married acquaintance, Forrest Footloose, has a great advantage over older investors. He has a lot of time to enjoy the extraordinary benefits of compounding. The earlier he decides to start, the better off compounding can make the result. Unfortunately, when we are in the Forrest Footloose stage there is a tendency to blow off investing with a belief that we have so much time ahead of us that there is no need to start right now. While there may not be a need, there is a fantastic advantage.

At Forrest's age (twentysomething) he may not have a lot of money to invest, but even a little can turn into a pretty sizeable pot with enough time ahead of him. Bonds may not be the most exciting vehicle for Forrest, but they can provide either current coupon income or a way to invest for the future. He could probably do better using a different strategy to produce current income (maybe covered calls or calendar spreads), but as a start at diversification he might do well to invest in some bonds or bond funds to begin to establish an ultimate nest egg. Something like TIPS in an IRA will inflation-proof that part of his portfolio and guarantee compounded growth over his 30 or so years to retirement.

Another thought might be to buy a bond fund in a 401(k) if offered as a possible asset. The inclusion of that kind of asset can help diversify the holdings and may act as a partial hedge against the stock portion of the portfolio.

Tim and Mary Middleton: Corporates for Yield or TIPS for Inflation Protection

The Middletons are at a stage where, though busy, they are becoming conscious of a need to preserve and grow capital. They may have some specific needs on a near or distant horizon and, as we discussed earlier, may not have a lot of time to devote to management of their investments.

Future obligations may be provided for with the purchase of zero coupons or TIPS for the inflation protection. I Bonds, too, might be considered as a way to set aside money for college, especially if the criteria to make the interest tax-free when used for educational purposes are met.

Since the Middletons are progressing into high earnings years, they may find themselves in a high tax bracket at which point it might be wise to consider the tax-free benefits of municipal bonds to add a stream of income while diversifying a portfolio. Taxable corporates with higher coupon yields and TIPS with inflation protection built-in might be considered for tax-advantaged accounts like IRAs.

Ed and Grace Balding: Laddering Treasuries with Inflation Protection

As the years pass, preservation of capital becomes more and more important. Ed and Grace have achieved that state. They need to create income while preserving capital and probably have more aversion to risk than

Forrest or the Middletons since it will be harder for them at advancing ages to make up for any losses.

Bonds with longer maturities have higher risk to principal until they mature than do shorter maturity bonds so unless the Baldings have an abundance of capital and are assured they will have no need for the principal before maturity, they may want to avoid the long-term bonds. Instead, one consideration might be a bond fund from which they can expect regular income without the risk of owning an individual issue or issues. In general, they can avoid credit risk by purchasing treasuries, but the notes and bonds do have interest rate risk so the Baldings would need to make sure they do not have a need for the principal until maturity.

Inflation can be an important consideration for people living on a fixed income so some might consider I Bonds or TIPS. Interest on the I Bonds will increase with inflation thereby enabling the owner to receive greater interest at times of greater inflation while running no risk of principal loss. TIPS protect the principal from inflation by adjusting the principal amount with movements in inflation, but since they can be traded in the secondary markets include the risk that some principal could be lost in the event they had to be sold before maturity. Using either or both these types of bonds, the Baldings might consider laddering in order to provide for regular distributions as needed.

 ■ **GETTING INTO GEAR**

I didn't investigate bonds until relatively late in life, but, even then, I'm really glad I did. Bonds offer a wide variety of possibilities from great safety and assured regular yields to inflation-protected investments to tax-free vehicles. Higher yields can generally be had when the investor is willing to take on higher risk. A bond portfolio can be structured so that the investor can provide income and/or capital at predetermined times. U.S. Government obligations are considered to be free of risk and the notes, bonds, and TIPS can be traded for capital gains (or losses) if the investor wants to be proactive.

These are investments that, once understood, can be entered and maintained with little time and effort. They can be used to produce current income or to provide for future needs. They can provide important diversification to any portfolio and may act as a hedge against an adverse movement in the stock portion of a portfolio as bonds often, though not always, move in a direction opposite to stocks.

Whether we are young or old or somewhere in between, bonds can have some attractive attributes and are worthy of inclusion in the portfolios of many smart investors.

CHAPTER 9

Annuities and Reverse Mortgages

Machines That Run on Their Own

I n this chapter, we'll look at a couple of ways to create streams of income with almost no effort once the initial investigations have been completed and a contract entered. Annuities and reverse mortgages each involve a contract and the use of already existing assets to set up an income flow. While the attributes of each of these devices differ as we'll see later in the chapter, one important factor they share is that neither requires any work on the part of the investor once put in place. All we need to do is sit back and receive the checks.

During the last half of my legal career, I was engaged in the defense of some heavy-duty personal injury cases. Often the people suing my client had suffered truly life-changing, catastrophic injuries that would prevent them from returning to their former jobs and, in some cases, to any job at all. In other cases, a widow might be making the claim after the death of her husband. Though lawsuits cannot restore a life or heal an injury, they do enable a successful claimant to obtain compensation for past and future loss of earnings, past and future medical costs, and past and future pain and suffering. In many of the cases I have handled, these amounts could be very significant.

Take a hypothetical situation where a man in his mid-twenties earning $40,000 a year doing physical work is so horribly injured that he will never be able to return to his occupation. He will only be able to work in a sedentary capacity and would need extensive training to find employment. His disabilities require major renovation of his home just so he can get around and attend to the functions of daily living. Even if he retrains and finds a suitable job, it appears he can only get a starting salary of about half of

135

what he is earning and there will be a disparity between what he can actually earn and what he would have earned in his former employment for the rest of his work life expectancy. His medical bills are astronomical and, in addition, he is expected to require at least two future surgeries and hospitalizations, the cost of which is estimated at $200,000 each. To top it all off, his wife is expecting their first child in a few months. Assuming that my client is likely to be held responsible for the injuries, it could be the subject of a multimillion-dollar judgment. Assuming that occurs, the young man who was so horribly injured would receive a large amount of cash (even after a 33 percent or 40 percent legal fee). He has no experience managing large sums of money and needs to use the money and whatever it might earn throughout the rest of his life. I have seen it happen where people in that situation have simply blown the money in a short amount of time and then are left with nothing. Fancy cars are purchased, money flows like water, and the fellow is lured into some scam investments or he gives his money over to some self-styled expert money manager who proceeds to lose a bundle. Unfortunately, the approach seems to be similar to that of many lottery winners who find themselves back to where they began within a couple of years of hitting the jackpot.

One way to attempt to avoid the problem is an annuity, but annuities certainly are not limited to settlements in large personal injury lawsuits. They can become an important element in creating retirement income or in planning for circumstances well into the future. A little later in the chapter, I'll suggest a way an annuity might be set up to settle the hypothetical claimant's lawsuit, but first I need to define an annuity.

WHAT IS AN ANNUITY?

An annuity is a contract between someone and an insurance company. In exchange for a payment or payments, the annuitant (usually also the owner) receives future payment or payments from the insurance company. There are at least two, and often three, phases to an annuity. In the first phase, sometimes called the accumulation phase, money is paid into the account with the insurance company. In the final phase, money is paid out to the annuitant according to the payout option chosen. Although annuities may begin paying out right after money is paid in, it is frequently the case that there is a middle phase during which the money is held in the account with the insurance company as it grows and compounds. Since the payments to the annuitant will be made in the future, the initial payment(s) to the insurance company will be earning and compounding over time so the payout to the annuitant will normally far exceed the initial investment. Generally, annuities offer tax-deferred growth since taxes are not levied on investments and income until money is actually withdrawn and it is then taxed at ordinary income tax rates.

Annuities come in various types (e.g., fixed, variable, combination of fixed and variable, and equity-indexed), with various benefits (e.g., death benefit), with almost infinite payout possibilities, and with various charges, all of which we'll explore in the sections that follow.

In lawsuits like the earlier hypothetical I have often counseled my client to offer a combination of cash plus annuity in settlement of the claim. Often, a responsible lawyer for the injured party agrees that an annuity may be a smart thing to do for his client. As a follow-up to the earlier hypothetical and to illustrate a variety of ways an annuity payout could be structured, my client might offer enough cash up front to satisfy the claimant's legal fees and costs plus several thousand dollars and, in addition, monthly payments for life of $2,000 a month increasing by 3 percent each year to account for inflation, plus a cash payment of $200,000 in three years and another in six years to pay for the anticipated surgeries, and beginning in 17 years four annual payments of $25,000 each to help with the soon-to-be-born baby's college education. All the monthly payments, the future medical payments, and the college fund would be paid through the annuity. If the offer were accepted, the injured person would have some degree of financial security to help him pay costs of living plus known, anticipated large future expenditures. He would not be burdened with the difficulties of managing a large amount of money without any training or experience and he would be less likely to fall prey to scam artists. From my client's point of view, the cost of buying an annuity to guarantee the payouts over the years would probably be significantly less than having to pay all the money up front, and the injured party would have an additional guarantee of payment because the annuity would have been purchased from a large insurance company.

The benefit of buying a future stream of income at today's prices is the primary financial enticement for my client. The money my client pays to the insurance company for the annuity then is paid out over time and since only a small portion is being paid out regularly, the remainder is earning so, through compounding principles, the payout will be much greater than the initial cost.

As an aside in the personal injury litigation arena, one development I have seen is that companies are now advertising that they cash out annuities originally paid to injured claimants. One of the main reasons for the claimant to have received an annuity is precisely to avoid the pitfalls of trying to manage large amounts of cash without enough knowledge; in plain words, to avoid blowing the money. By selling the annuity for cash, these folks are doing precisely what they were trying to avoid in the first place. While some may simply have no choice because of some urgent need for cash, I suspect most are just interested in getting a fairly large lump. If the latter situation is the case, one can only hope that they have gained some knowledge and experience in money management and are not simply setting themselves up for failure.

TYPES OF ANNUITIES

Fixed Annuity

When selling a fixed annuity, the insurance company makes a couple of guarantees. First, it guarantees that your annuity account will earn a minimum interest rate during the period when the account is growing, and, second, it guarantees that the payout of periodic payments will be at least a specific minimum for each dollar in the account. Fixed annuities are not securities and, therefore, are not regulated by the Securities and Exchange Commission as of the time of this writing.

Variable Annuity

As is the case with any annuity, the first phase of the contract between the owner and an insurance company is the payment or payments made into the account. The owner then normally chooses from among an array of mutual funds where the money will be invested. Depending on the contract, the investment could be in bonds, large caps, small caps, mid-caps, money markets, specific industries, foreign securities, real estate, or combinations of those investments. Performance of the overall annuity investment will be dependent on the specific investment choices made.

Suppose, for example, that we decided to buy a variable annuity for $10,000 and chose to invest 40 percent in large caps, 40 percent in small caps, and 20 percent in bonds. If the large caps had a return of 8 percent, the small caps a return of 15 percent, and the bonds a return of 4 percent, at the end of the year the account (before charges) would look like this:

$$\text{Large cap portion} = \$4,320 \ (\$10,000 \times 40 \text{ percent}$$
$$= \$4,000 + 8 \text{ percent})$$
$$\text{Small cap portion} = \$4,600 \ (\$10,000 \times 40 \text{ percent}$$
$$= \$4,000 + 15 \text{ percent})$$
$$\text{Bond portion} = \$2,080 \ (\$10,000 \times 20 \text{ percent}$$
$$= \$2,000 + 4 \text{ percent})$$
$$\text{Total value at year end} = \$11,000$$

In most cases, at least until the payout phase, we can change the investments or the percentages allocated to the investments though fees may be incurred for the transfers.

Once the payout phase is reached with any annuity contract whether it be fixed, variable, a combination, or equity-indexed, there usually is a wide array of possibilities from which the annuitant may select. The possibilities are governed by the specific terms of each annuity contract so the buyer should be sure to investigate those alternatives before buying the annuity in the first place. A review of the prospectus will set out the terms of the annuity. In general, though, with variable annuities as with the other types, the annuitant can take the payment in a lump sum or through periodic payments. Depending on needs the annuitant may take a lump sum distribution and roll it into a new annuity to again seek tax-deferred gains. If current income is the goal, the annuitant may choose to take periodic payments each month or each year. The periodic payments may be guaranteed for a specific period such as 20 or 30 years or they may be based on the life of the annuitant or perhaps by the longer of the lives of the annuitant and his spouse. Combinations may be created where the payout is payable to the annuitant or spouse for life, 10 years certain. That means that the annuity payments will continue until the last surviving spouse passes on but that payments will be made for at least 10 years even if both die before the expiration of 10 years. As we saw in the hypothetical personal injury example, the payout may be structured so that certain larger payments are made at specific future dates to cover expected future expenses.

Quite often, variable annuities include a death benefit that guarantees payment of a specific amount to beneficiaries if you die before the payouts have begun. Ordinarily, the guaranteed death benefit is at least equal to the amount(s) you paid to purchase the annuity.

In addition to the distribution options and the death benefit, variable annuities like the other types offer the significant benefit of tax-deferred gains. From initial accumulation until payout begins, no taxes are paid on the gains as they accrue. I should note that buying a variable annuity in a tax-advantaged plan such as an IRA or 401(k) offers no additional tax advantage and for the majority of investors, it is probably better to max out their IRA or 401(k) contributions before considering the purchase of an annuity. However, as with all major investments, it is best to obtain the advice of a tax professional before making any final decisions.

Combination Fixed and Variable Annuity

I do include an annuity among my own investments. It is a combination fixed and variable annuity. Principal is guaranteed along with the guarantee of a 7 percent per year return for 10 years of accumulation. The contract also provides the ability to choose among various investments so that I enjoy the benefits if those investments exceed the guaranteed 7 percent per year. That provision enables me to select some high-potential but speculative investment categories since even under a worst-case scenario, the annuity earns 7 percent a year, which means that the initial investment should approximately double in 10 years.[*] If the investments do better, the fund will double more quickly.

My combined fixed and variable annuity also includes a death benefit that assures payment of at least my contributions to my beneficiaries in the event of what I certainly would consider to be my premature death.

Although I haven't reached an age or station where I would be interested in receiving an annuity payout, as I was writing this section I checked to see approximately what monthly payment I could receive at age 75 if my wife were then 65 and I bought an annuity at that point for $500,000. According to one chart, if the payout were based on the longer of both our lives and was guaranteed to be paid for at least 10 years whether we lived that long or not, the payment would be a little more than $3,000 a month. This scenario is only an example, and by the time I hit 75 if I make it that far, the number will most likely be different since the payout is related to interest rates at the time. When interest rates are high, a specific amount of cash could be expected to buy a higher payout while when rates are low the payout would likely be reduced. Once the payout is set, however, in most cases it will remain at that level regardless of where interest rates may go from there.

Equity-Indexed Annuity

Equity-indexed annuities earn interest that is linked to some equity index such as the S&P 500 Composite Index. Performance is linked to the index with these annuities just as it would be linked to selected mutual funds in a variable annuity, but there is an important distinction in that equity-indexed annuities also have a guaranteed minimum return. As a result of the guarantee, these are generally considered to be fixed annuities.

Probably the most important feature of these equity-based annuities is the guarantee that your account will not go below what you paid plus any accrued interest no matter what the index to which it is tied may do. As I noted in the previous section, the combination annuity I own has a similar provision.

---

[*]Using the so-called Rule of 72 whereby the number 72 is divided by the rate of compounded interest to approximate the number of years in which the fund will double. In this case $72 \div 7 = 10.3$ years.

It is relatively important to be aware that depending on a specific contract the account may actually be credited with a smaller gain than the actual return of the index to which it is linked. Some equity-indexed annuities, for example, may have provisions that apply an upper limit to the rate of interest that may be earned.

In short, these annuities can be relatively complicated and as with all annuities, the buyer should review the prospectus and consult with a professional tax advisor before choosing a specific product.

CONSIDERATIONS FOR ANNUITY INVESTORS

Risks

Undoubtedly the first and most important risk an annuity buyer encounters is the strength of the insurance company with which he may be contracting. An annuity is worthless if the insurance company isn't around or doesn't have the assets to make the payouts when the time comes. Until the melt-down beginning in 2008, we felt reasonably comfortable buying an annuity from almost any large well-known insurance company, but the troubles of behemoth AIG and the attempted government bailout must give pause before entering a contract even with the giants. Nothing will ever be completely safe so we must investigate the assets and ratings of a particular insurance company and then make our best judgment on the basis of the information at hand. Accrual requirements by governmental entities should also be investigated particularly where the annuity contains a life insurance provision since they may give added protection.

Variable annuities have the additional risk that the investments we choose in our account may perform poorly and unless there is a minimum guarantee, the account value could fall.

Fixed annuities and equity-indexed annuities may present the risk of lost opportunity in that we might do better by investing elsewhere and achieving a rate higher than the annuity is achieving.

Charges and Penalties

One of the most significant potential charges with an annuity is the surrender charge. That is a charge paid to the insurance company if money is withdrawn before a specified period of time has passed (sometimes as long as 10 years). The charge can be fairly hefty if money is withdrawn early and the earlier the withdrawal, the higher the charge. In the early years, the charge might be as much as 8 percent or 9 percent of the withdrawal and in most cases we can expect to see the percentage diminish with the passage of time. Unless the money is withdrawn to be exchanged for another annuity, it will also likely be a taxable event and may be subject to a penalty as well. If the transaction is to exchange one annuity for another it is what is known as a 1035 exchange and is tax-free though it may still be subject to surrender charges if the first annuity has not been held long enough to go past the required period.

For those reasons, the annuity must be treated as a long-term investment. Surrender charges make annuities unsuitable for short-term investments and can result in significant losses if money is withdrawn before the surrender period has passed. When buying an annuity, the purchaser should be reasonably certain that he will not need the money at least until the surrender charge period has passed.

The annuity account is also subject to administrative fees and fees that pay the insurance company for risks it assumes under the contract (sometimes known as the mortality risk). Beyond that, with a variable annuity the account also indirectly pays the charges levied by the mutual funds that comprise the chosen investments.

Suitability

As always, the question becomes whether the investment is suitable for you, the individual. Annuities essentially provide a hands-off investment that offers some level of security particularly if principal and some minimum rate of return is guaranteed. They may be attractive to investors who do not have the time or do not want to be involved with management of all or a portion of their assets. They offer an advantage of tax-deferred growth of professionally managed money and a steady stream of income for the annuitant once payout begins.

Would an annuity be attractive to someone like our old buddy, Forrest Footloose? Though some may suggest that younger investors like Forrest might be better off with higher risk investments, a regular program of investing in annuities for the long haul could lead to significant retirement income with little effort. For example, if Forrest could invest $5,000 at age 25 and $10,000 every 10 years after that, he could have a lump of over $200,000 by age 65.

The Middletons might also want to diversify a bit as cash became more available and create an annuity that would help as they approached retirement. Oftentimes, parents of folks like the Middletons pass on leaving the children an inheritance. It might be reasonable for them to consider buying an annuity with some of that windfall to avoid blowing it, particularly if they don't have the time or desire to manage other more time-consuming investments.

Quite often, retirees like the Baldings may consider annuities to convert part of a nest egg to regular lifetime income. As age advances, the Baldings may prefer the rocker to dealing with investment activity and an annuity can give them some assurance that they won't outlive their money since they will have some guaranteed income throughout their lives.

I am a believer in diversification and annuities can help diversify assets. They also can be valuable in situations where someone does not understand investing and money management, does not want to manage money, or is physically or mentally incapable of managing investments. While annuities may not offer the most lucrative possibilities, they can have an important place in achieving some degree of financial security with little effort once the investment has been entered.

REVERSE MORTGAGES

These devices are reserved for the older crowd and have recently gained fairly widespread popularity. Reverse mortgages exist for those who have equity in a home that they want to convert to income. Although they actually are a loan where debt is rising and equity falling, reverse mortgages do have some attractive features. Though I am generally opposed to debt especially as we get older, debt creation usually involves borrowing money that hasn't yet been earned, but in the case of reverse mortgages, we have already earned the equity against which we are borrowing. Normally when we borrow against a home with a traditional mortgage the home is at risk if we are unable to make the payments as so many learned with the financial crisis beginning in 2007. That is not the case with the reverse mortgage since we have no obligation to make payments.

What Is a Reverse Mortgage?

Quite simply, a reverse mortgage is a specific type of home loan that enables a homeowner to convert equity into cash. However, it differs significantly from a traditional mortgage, second mortgage, or home-equity loan in that it does not need to be repaid until the borrower or borrowers no longer use the home as their principal residence, and no matter how much the borrower has been paid, repayment cannot exceed the value of the home so other assets are not at risk to satisfy the reverse mortgage loan.

Requirements

Reverse mortgages currently are not available to everyone. In order to obtain a reverse mortgage, the borrowers must all be over 62 years of age and must own their home. Only the principal residence (the one where we live more than half the year) can be the subject of the loan, and in most cases the residence must be a single-family dwelling, a two- to four-unit building, or an approved condo or PUD (planned unit development). Additionally, the home must be free and clear or any existing mortgage must be satisfied before the reverse mortgage is created. Since you are still the owner of your home after the reverse mortgage is in effect, you are still responsible for items like property taxes, insurance, and maintenance.

Benefits to the Homeowner

The first reason to consider a reverse mortgage is the receipt of cash. Several payment options are available. The homeowners could elect monthly payments for as long as the home remains their principal residence (which could be as long as until the death of the last surviving owner), or a lump sum payment, or a line of credit. No matter what alternative is chosen, as long as the owners pay the taxes, keep up the property, and continue to use the home as their principal residence, they do not have to repay the loan. Once the home is no longer used as the principal residence, whether as a result of sale, moving, or death, the actual amount paid the owners together with interest and fees must be repaid, but, very significantly, no matter what the size of the loan, the amount that must be repaid cannot exceed the value of the house at that time. In other words, if a spouse should happen to live well beyond her normal life expectancy and was receiving monthly payments her whole life so that the payments greatly exceeded the value of the house, the most that would have to be repaid would be the value of the house and the loan holder could not look to any other assets to satisfy the loan.

Once again, I would counsel the reader to check with a tax professional to confirm the tax information set out below before acting, but as of this writing the IRS does not consider loan advances (the payments made to the homeowners in a reverse mortgage) to be income. Importantly, then, the payment or payments received by the owners are free of income taxation. The money received is, therefore, all spendable. Before electing whether to take a lump sum or monthly payments, a property owner could check to see what monthly payment he could buy in an annuity using a lump sum payment from the reverse mortgage versus what he would receive in monthly payments on the reverse mortgage itself. Annuity advances may be at least partially taxable. It is worth noting that while the payments may not be considered as income for tax purposes, interest that is being charged is not deductible until it is actually paid so though it is accruing, interest cannot be deducted until the loan is ultimately repaid.

Since there sometimes may be confusion as to whether the lender gets your house at the end of the loan, I want to make it clear that the lender gets nothing more than repayment of the loan, plus interest, plus any fees or costs. If the house has value greater than the loan, it does not go to the lender. Any value in excess of the loan goes to you or your heirs, not to the lender.

At least for now, Social Security and Medicare benefits are unaffected by reverse mortgage payments though the Supplemental Security Income and Medicaid benefits may well be affected. Once again, it is important to check out your personal situation with a professional before acting.

Costs

As with almost all loans, the lender is charging interest. In the case of a reverse mortgage, the interest is not being paid out; rather it is accruing against the loan amount and is something that must be repaid when the home ceases to be a principal residence. As noted earlier, no matter how high the loan balance has risen, including the interest, the lender is limited to recovering no more than the value of the home at the time the loan is repaid.

In addition to interest, other costs may also be included in the loan. They might include things like origination fees, survey and title charges, inspection fees, recording fees, and the like.

Federal law requires reverse mortgage lenders to disclose the projected annual average cost of the loans in a manner that includes all costs and benefits. This TALC (Total Annual Loan Cost) discloses the total cost and interest you are paying for the money you are receiving from the lender.

Other Considerations

Though it is beyond the scope of this book and in light of an ongoing financial crisis at the time of this writing, the reader should at least be aware that there are a couple of types of reverse mortgages. One alternative is the federally insured HECM (Home Equity Conversion Mortgage) while another is what is known as Fannie Mae's HomeKeeper. Anyone considering a reverse mortgage should investigate the differences in the costs and requirements of these alternatives through a professional before taking action.

 GETTING INTO GEAR

In this chapter we have explored a couple of avenues through which an investor might create additional streams of income with little or no effort once the initial due diligence has been performed.

Annuities may be attractive to investors in a variety of situations ranging from those just entering their earnings years to those reaching retirement. They can provide a guaranteed stream of income through the remainder of an investor's life with no action on his part after purchase other than endorsing the check. They require little or no management and have the advantage of deferring taxes on their growth. In general, annuities must be considered to be long-term investments since penalties for withdrawals before the end of the accumulation phase can be very onerous.

Reverse mortgages are only available to the older generation (62 or greater) and enable the "investor" to turn home equity into an income stream. I put quotes around "investor" since a reverse mortgage creates a debt that ultimately must be repaid. Older homeowners, however, can stay in their homes throughout their lives and receive monthly payments from the lender with no obligation to do anything until the home is no longer their principal residence. In other words, health permitting, they can live in their home until death and only then will the loan have to be repaid, but repayment is limited to the value of the house at that time. If money is left over from the sale of the house after the lender is repaid the loan with interest and costs, the remainder is the property of the owner or his heirs.

Each of these strategies can be beneficial to those who don't have the time or inclination to become involved in active investing. Though investors may give up the potential of greater rewards, annuities and reverse mortgages can provide money flow with at least a modicum of security.

CHAPTER 10

Running the Money Machine

I n the preceding chapters, we've touched on at least 14 different methods[*] by which the smart investor can create additional streams of income. These are all parts that may be used in the creation of your own money machine. Though there is absolutely no need for any individual to use them all there are probably many reasons why almost anyone reading this book might want to use one or more of them. The strategies and methods run a gamut from safe to risky and from methods requiring a lot of attention to others that require almost none. Many of the strategies can be used by people in every age group and at almost every economic level. All the strategies have one desirable thing in common: they can add a stream of income to your life.

Of course, there is no way to run the money machine until we build it. Now is the time for the decision I talked about back in Chapter 2. We either decide to build the machine or we decide to continue along as we have without enjoying the added income it can provide. There may be valid reasons why we might not be able to start immediately, but we have to

---

[*]Buying dividend producing stocks, writing covered calls, call calendar spreads, LEAPS strategies, REITs, MLPs, vertical spreads, iron condors, naked puts, naked straddles, naked strangles, bonds, annuities, and reverse mortgages.

be careful that they are not just excuses. The two questions I think we should ask ourselves are:

1. Do I want added income?
2. Now that I know a lot of ways to add income streams, why shouldn't I build a money machine for myself?

Naturally the answer to the first question will almost always be a resounding "Yes!" The real question is whether there is some reason to talk ourselves out of building the machine. If we can't build a money machine because we don't have the time, we could use strategies that don't require much, if any, time. We also should do a little self-examination and see whether we might rearrange a little of our time to enable us to spend some time working on the machine. After all, a little work on adding streams of income should free up more time in the future.

If the reason we can't build the money machine is that we don't have any money to start with, maybe it is worth going back to the old-fashioned concept of tightening our belt a little and saving a bit to invest. All too often, credit card debt has prevented people from making investments. Their existing income is eaten away by debt service. Many people have used credit and are now paying 18 percent or more a year in interest. With $10,000 of debt, that's $1,800 a year down the tubes. Doesn't it only make good sense to reduce and get rid of the debt? How can it be done? Pay more than the minimum payment and stop adding to the credit card debt. I know that almost seems un-American, but until the debt is satisfied, the boulder will remain on our chest. Even though we may have a rush of instant gratification when we buy something now instead of waiting, what have we really accomplished? We will pay much more for the article because of the credit card interest than we would pay if we waited, and we will continue to prevent ourselves from having the money to invest to create more income.

It is always our choice. We can build a money machine or not. If we do, the financial quality of our lives can be better, in many cases a lot better. If we don't, the likelihood is that we will never get where we would like to be. I once heard a great trading instructor teach that, "if you are willing to do for a year what others won't, you will be able to do for the rest of your life what others can't." It's up to you.

I chose to build the machine. I've personally used all the strategies about which I've written here (except the reverse mortgage) and they provide my living. For those people who do want to build their machine, in the following sections, I've set out a number of important things I've learned over my trading years that may help you along the way.

If you have decided that you are going to build a money machine, do it for yourself (and your family). I put "and your family" in parentheses because they will benefit from the results. The machine, itself, has to be for you because you must build one you like, one that you want, one that fits your personality, one that you can comfortably manage. Unless your machine fits within those parameters you won't be happy and if you aren't happy, it won't be the best machine for you.

A good starting point in your decision-making process might be to assess how much time you have available and how much you are willing to devote to the construction and maintenance of your machine. If you are really interested in trading and have several hours a week available, you might look at trading spreads or naked puts. On the other hand, if you aren't really interested in trading and have hardly any time at all but are looking for added income down the road when you slow down, you might consider an annuity. For some people, a combination of a little trading like writing covered calls against an existing portfolio while also buying some shares of a MLP might work. My best advice is to only commit to as much time as is comfortable for you.

As we have seen, and as I addressed in some detail in *Trade Your Way to Wealth*, various strategies carry widely diverse risk. Buying stock, for example, can be risky since a stock can go to zero. U.S. Government Bonds are considered to be as safe as it gets. The sky is the limit on the potential reward for the stockowner while in some cases the bondholder will have a gain limited to interest earned. We need to determine a comfortable, realistic reward to risk parameter for our machine. When creating the blueprint, some serious self-examination is necessary. What really is your risk tolerance? Ordinarily, we perceive a higher risk tolerance when things are looking good, but, in reality, when things are going against us, our tolerance is not nearly as great as we may have thought. Honest self-appraisal is important. Consider how much you can lose without the necessity of a change in lifestyle and when you have that answer ask yourself exactly how much of that amount you really would be willing to lose.

I have only three criteria in deciding whether to use a particular strategy at some specific time:

1. Do I like it?
2. Does it appear to offer a suitable risk to reward possibility?
3. Does it appear to fit current market conditions?

If you like the strategy, it simply means does it pass a "gut check"? That is relatively subjective. Whether it appears to offer a suitable risk to reward depends on the strategy. If I am buying a dividend paying stock, for example, I would not only look to the dividend yield, but also to where I would sell to cut losses and where it looked like it could go to an initial target. If it looked like the risk to reward was 2.5:1 or better, I would also consider it to be acceptable from a risk to reward standpoint. By appearing to fit market conditions, it simply means that I want a strategy appropriate to what is currently going on in the market. I would want to use a bearish strategy in a bearish market (like a bear call spread), a bullish strategy in a bullish market (like buying a stock or writing covered calls or selling naked puts), or a neutral strategy in a neutral market (like iron condors or naked strangles).

If I like it, it fits the market, and the risk to reward looks decent, what more would I need. Naturally, for all of us if we are trading, we may and should change strategies from time to time as market conditions warrant.

TRADE IN THE PRESENT

Recently a subscriber to my newsletter wrote to say that the best trading advice usually doesn't sound like trading advice. I think that was an extraordinarily perceptive observation.

In classes, in coaching sessions, and in discussions with traders I have repeatedly seen attempts to predict what will happen. "Earnings are going to come in great," someone will say or "I know XYZ is going to $80," from someone else. It is an interesting exercise that is impossible to achieve over time. As you read, ask yourself questions like: Will there be a catastrophic world event tomorrow? Will a major drug company announce the cure for cancer this week? Clearly, any attempted answer would be pure speculation yet that is what so many traders and investors try to do. They try to predict the future. Whether there is a catastrophic world event tomorrow would certainly have an effect on the markets. If you had been bullish such an event could certainly change your perspective. Perhaps a buy-and-hold investor would hang onto bullish positions, but a trader might well act to cut losses promptly and, perhaps, switch to a bearish strategy. It is clear that we are simply not able to predict the future with any significant degree of reliability, but many people keep trying.

The past is gone and we can't know the future so the only place we can act is in the present. I didn't make up the saying. We've all heard it before, we know it's true, yet we seem to pay no attention since we are forever trying to predict the future. About a third of most newscasts are devoted to the weather forecast and how do they do with that?

When we turn to our investments and our trading, we must work in the present if we are going succeed. As they say, we are always on the right side of the chart and although we may have some information that may suggest a stock is more likely to go in a particular direction, it is no guarantee. What will XYZ do tomorrow? If we look at a chart, we may see that it has been moving up in price and looks like it could go another $3 until it reached a point where it had turned down before (a resistance). At the same time we can see that the support (or floor where it had last reversed and turned up) was $1 down from here. Now we may think this stock is going to go up, but we know it could also go down. What can we do? How about buy the stock? We have a risk to reward potential of 3:1 so if we are wrong, we lose $1 a share and if we are right we make at least $3 a share. Does it matter what the stock does? Sure, for this play, but we have set ourselves up so that if we are right only half the time we are still going to make money. We're making $3 for every $1 we lose. That is a simplification of using a risk to reward strategy to attempt to profit even when we know we are going to be wrong sometimes.

In the example, we used the uptrend in the stock price as a clue that it might continue to go up but we were aware that it also could go down as soon as we bought the stock. What made the play attractive was that we saw a potential upside that was three times greater than the potential downside. Acting in the present, we saw a way to construct a trade so that even if there was a 50/50 chance of success, the potential reward would be three times greater than the loss and we would take steps (like a stop-loss order) to assure our loss would be limited to $1 a share.

I can't tell you how often I've heard students, other traders, and even myself at times say: "I think it'll (go up, go down, fill in the blank)." We need to realize that what we think it will do has absolutely no influence whatsoever on what it will do. It doesn't know what we think, and if it did, it wouldn't care. We must combat our propensity to think something will act in a specific way by planning ahead. Find a target at the upside resistance and find a support level on the downside and make sure it fits your risk to reward requirements and then plan the trade to exit and cut the loss if it hits the downside support. Once the price hits the upside target, trail a stop behind so you don't take yourself out prematurely. Each of those steps is performed in the now. We can place all the orders at the same time or we can predetermine our points of action like when the loss is to be cut and when and how profits are to be captured and act as those points are hit. The decisions have all been made in the present and that is where we need to be.

DEVELOP SELF-DISCIPLINE

We all have a little voice in us that makes suggestions, particularly about trading, I think. The voice certainly seems to me to be that of an emotion. "You better get out, this could turn the other way," it may say. Or how about: "I think it will turn back up to where I bought it if I just hang on"?

In the first case the voice could be encouraging us to cut our profits; in the second, it urges us to let our losses run. Those thoughts are exactly backward of what we should be doing, but I daresay most of us have not only heard, but have also acted on the suggestion. Logically, our trading decision may be indefensible, but emotionally, it is right on the mark.

Trading has a strong and undeniable emotional component. While we may never be able to eliminate all the emotion (and we probably wouldn't want to) it is important that we keep the emotions under control in our trading. If we are going to be successful, we must develop self-discipline. Entering the trade should not be the first step. Entry is the second step taken only after we have constructed our plan for the entire trade. That means that our exit strategy and how it will be accomplished is in place before we ever enter a position.

As an example, suppose we have decided we like XYZ. It is trading at $30 a share. There is an apparent support at $29, and the next area of resistance is around $33. We can see that the potential risk to reward is about 3:1 so it would meet my criteria that I want to see a risk to reward of at least 2.5 to 1. If I bought shares at $30, I would attempt to cap my loss at $1 a share by placing a stop loss (or an alert to get out) around $29. I would also place an alert to be notified when the price hit about $32.75 with a plan to raise my stop up close behind so that I would be taken out with a profit if the resistance held at $33. Once the stock got above $33, I would place a trailing stop maybe 2 percent behind the move. That would mean that if the stock dipped 2 percent from whatever new highs it might make my shares would then be sold automatically. At that point, unless there was a gap down, I would be assured of a profit and more and more profit would be accumulating as long as the move continued without a 2 percent drop from the high. That might be my plan. As you can see, the contingencies are accounted for; my initial stop-loss order(s) can be placed when I enter the position and if I am not stopped out at $29, I know when to take the next action and exactly what that action is going to be. Now, although the emotion and the little voice may remain, the trade has been accomplished from beginning to end in a disciplined manner. All I have to do is make sure my emotions are not permitted to override the plan no matter how loud they scream.

BE WILLING TO CUT LOSSES AND LET PROFITS RUN

I mentioned these important principles in the preceding section, but they are of such critical importance that they definitely deserve a section of their own. It is as simple as this: good traders cut their losses and let their profits run; bad traders don't. Unfortunately, many retail traders do exactly the opposite of what they should. They cut their profits and let their losses run. I am convinced that those unsuccessful folks listen to and are controlled by the little voice.

So often I have heard tales of woe from investors who held a stock with no exit plan as it began a decline. At the first point of concern, they decide they will sell at a specific point, but when the stock drops below that point, they decide to let it go a little further. "It'll come back," says the voice. It doesn't turn back, it keeps dropping, and they decide if it just gets back to that point where they first said they'd sell it, they'll get out. On it goes until finally, totally exasperated, they just sell it. Naturally, Murphy's Law takes over and the stock immediately starts back up. In any event, letting a stock drop just another nickel or dime or dollar, or saying "It'll come back" are ways in which we let our losses run. I seriously suggest investors avoid that syndrome. Plan your exit so that you do have a set exit if the stock turns against you. Cut the loss! If the stock turns back up, get back in, but don't ride the position to the bottom.

One thing I have regularly observed in working with my coaching students and in speaking with seminar attendees is that serious students generally do learn to cut most losses fairly quickly. It seems like it is much more difficult to train ourselves to let profits run. There is a strong tendency to grab a profit as soon as it appears and, in many cases, that can result in cutting profits. The old saying is "You can't go broke taking a profit," but the corollary to that may be that you can't get rich taking profits prematurely. That is one reason why I will frequently place a percentage trailing stop behind an uptrending stock I may own. As long as it doesn't retrace more than the percentage I choose from the high, I remain in the play and am not tempted to sell and run the minute it makes some normal retracement.

KEEP LEARNING

I write a free weekly newsletter for MarketFn.com, a subscription service. While I am compensated for editing the paid services, I write the newsletter for no compensation. Unlike many of the other market newsletters, mine is not meant to be a market commentary; rather, it is designed to pass on knowledge about strategies, methods, approaches, and market psychology. I write it because I believe that all traders and investors can profit through enhancing their knowledge.

Unfortunately, a trading education can be difficult to obtain. While universities may offer financially related courses, it is relatively rare to find one on trading. Most individuals I know who have become either successful active traders and/or investors have had to educate themselves. I include myself in that group. From the time I first was exposed to some trading strategies, I was passionate to gain knowledge. I first saw that I didn't have to buy and hold for 20 or 30 years; in my case, it was too late for that. Instead I saw ways I could pay my bills at the end of the month and create streams of income from investments rather than from the sale of my time. Adding income made sense to me. I was convinced I could improve the quality of my life if I learned more about trading and investing so I became passionate about the subject. I read every trading book I could get my hands on and I attended seminar after seminar. As in every field, I found many things were useful and learned that some were scams and get-rich-quick schemes. I immersed myself in learning what looked to be valuable and rejected that which didn't. I continue the pattern today. I devote time each week to study and, for me, it has paid off.

A newsletter subscriber once wrote me that he didn't want to be scammed so he wasn't going to pay for any seminars, books, or DVDs. He was going to learn it on his own. Incredible, I thought. I can assure the reader that there likely is a no more expensive education than to try to learn trading and investing by trial and error. I would guess that the investment account will be empty long before the brain has enough information to become successful.

Once again, since you have read this far, I am probably preaching to the choir. You have made a decision to try to gain some knowledge by reading this book. You paid good hard-earned money to try to advance your knowledge and hopefully you have found something here that will help you cut a loss or ride a gain that makes investment in this part of your education worthwhile.

Penny wise and pound foolish is a concept that can be critically important to investors. If you decide that something is expensive and reject it for that reason, it may well be a foolish decision. In my own case, many years ago, I went to a free come-on seminar with my mind made up that I would not buy the seminar they would be selling. I knew it would be too expensive. In fact, back in the 1990s it was almost $4,000 for a two and a half day seminar and that was about 8 percent of my liquid net worth. For once, the little voice in my head did the right thing and I signed up, paid the $4,000, and went to the seminar. The seminar ended at noon on a Saturday and by about the following Tuesday I had made back the cost using information I had gained about trading at those classes. Trading became my livelihood from that time on. As I look back, I see that what looked like it was too expensive turned out to be the best investment I ever made. In retrospect, I would have been foolish not to spend the $4,000. Nowadays, when I consider the cost of some trading-related event or education, I just ask myself whether it can pay for itself in a trade or two either by showing me a way to limit a loss or by realizing a gain. In other words, what I am suggesting is an evaluation of how something may help rather than focusing solely on what it will cost. Not long ago, I had a fellow sign up for personal coaching with me. My charge was $3,000 for a day devoted to him and his individual trading. He had been trading for several years, but had been losing for a while. He voiced a great deal of concern and reluctance to pay $3,000 for a day, but ultimately decided to sign on. We spent what I considered to be a productive day and by day's end he was very pleased. In a week or so, he e-mailed me describing a trade he had opened and just closed following our time together. He was elated. He had realized a gain of $3,000 in a single trade by utilizing the principles we had discussed. Was it worth it? Only he could say. One thing is for certain. That fellow learned something new about trading and about himself.

Back in the early days of my own trading education, I was dedicated to learning strategies. I wanted to learn ways I could play positions that were going up, going down, or going sideways. There are wonderful strategies for each of those directions, but as I learned, there is a great deal more to investing than just knowing strategies. I have met many people who know more strategies than I do, but who are, nevertheless, unsuccessful. There are important steps to successful investing beyond simply knowing strategies though knowing strategies is an important part of the process.

Once we understand a strategy and what it is designed to do, it becomes important to learn when to exit or how to adjust the strategy in the event we are wrong about the direction of our choice. Many times over the years, I have entered a bullish option spread, for example, only to see the stock turn bearish. In at least some of those cases, I have been able to make adjustments and wind up with a profit greater than I would have made had the play worked out as initially designed.

Another subscriber to the newsletter once made what I considered to be a very profound observation. He suggested that some of the best trading advice we can get doesn't sound like trading advice. I agree. Trading advice sounds like when to buy a stock or when to sell a covered call or how to create an iron condor, but those things are only a part of the puzzle. I am convinced that a much more important part is self-knowledge and awareness. Successful trading in my view is much more recognition of the psychological than it is logical.

PRACTICE WHAT YOU LEARN

If you are interested in trading stock or options, it will be helpful to paper trade a strategy that you are learning. By paper trading, I mean practice the strategy using real market numbers without using real money. Some brokerage firms include the ability to make virtual trades on their web sites and to place real orders that will be executed with play money. I am convinced that paper trading is a very valuable exercise because it enables the student to learn a strategy and adjustments to the strategy well. The practice can help achieve a more complete understanding of how things might go as the market or a stock price moves over time. Since no money is at risk there is no danger of financial loss.

However, the student should be aware that because there is no risk of financial loss there is little real emotion involved in paper trading. We need to understand that paper trading is not like real money trading. I have met lots of traders who were highly successful paper traders but who fell flat when they tried to trade real money. What happened? When they started trading real money after their paper trading experience, they stopped what they had been doing. They no longer followed the rules they were following in their paper trades. The little voice in their heads took over and their trading became influenced by emotion. Placing money at risk is a very emotional act. Greed and fear arrive on the scene and we have trouble maintaining the needed discipline.

Some people argue that paper trading has no value because it is different from trading real money. I disagree. The key, in my estimation, is to understand that the two are very different so don't expect the same results in real money trading as you got paper trading unless you are doing the same things; following the same rules. The value of paper trading is to learn strategies well and to understand that you can be successful. Once those elements have been accomplished it is essential to understand that we can only expect to achieve similar results in real money trading if we apply the same rules and discipline to the real money trading as we did to our virtual trades.

DIVERSIFICATION

Throughout this book we have been investigating a variety of ways to produce streams of income. We can start with one new stream and as time passes change it to another stream or we can add streams to create a new river of income. As we proceed with our plan, and consider adding streams, I am a proponent of diversifying to spread risk. When I talk about diversifying, I mean more than buying stocks in different companies or different sectors. Buying stock in different sectors definitely is a form of diversification, but it is a beginning only. When I talk about diversification, I mean diversifying into different classes of assets. Owning a dividend-paying stock and selling a covered call might be one class that could be combined with bond ownership and, perhaps an annuity along with a Master Limited Partnership. A distribution of investments along those lines, for example, would give broader coverage among classes whose performance is not necessarily correlated. Each of those investments could be supplying an income stream but the performance of each class would not necessarily be correlated with any other so we might expect a flattening of overall risk as one class might grow as another might diminish.

An important factor in diversification is spreading risk. That concept also encompasses what I consider to be a crucial element in investing and that is money management. There are a number of ways to manage investment money, but it is important to be aware of the concept and choose one. The investor might decide to make equal dollar investments, for example. That enables him to spread equal amounts in different income producing asset classes. When I coach trading students, I suggest they consider equal percentage investments. Of course, in those cases we are usually talking about investing risk money in specific stock or option positions, but the concept is worthy of consideration in making any investment decisions. Investing equal percentages simply means that we identify our investment capital and divide it by equal percentage. As an example, we might decide we want to invest 25 percent in four classes of assets. Perhaps we would put 25 percent into dividend paying stocks, 25 percent into an annuity, 25 percent into REITs, and 25 percent into option trading. We could then take each segment and further divide it into equal percentages within the class. In our option trades, we could decide to place 5 percent of the money assigned to that class at risk in each trade. Suppose we started with $20,000 in our option trading investments. The first trade would risk 5 percent or $1,000. If that trade was a total loss, our option account would now be $19,000 so the next trade would risk 5 percent of that or $950 and if that trade made $3,000, our account would now be $22,000 and the next trade would risk $1,100. In other words, as our account increased, so, too, would the size of our trades and as the account value dipped, so, too, would the size of our trades.

The important thing about money management is that it keeps us in investments. We are never putting it all at risk in any one position and that adds an important element of risk reduction while permitting us to continue investing even if we suffer some losses. A different approach can lead to sad results. Years ago, I had a student who became a very successful trader. He was trading regularly for a while and enjoying exceptional results. He was following his money management plan and adding substantially to his account. The time came, however, when he stopped contacting me. I was concerned and called him only to find that after several successes in a row trading options on a specific stock he invested all his account in the next play. Success was dependent on the stock going up; instead, it gapped down significantly and he was wiped out. He was out of the game completely. Had he continued to utilize his original money management plan (5 percent of risk money per trade) he would have lost 5 percent but could have continued to trade, presumably with the same degree of success he had formerly enjoyed.

SELF-AWARENESS

If there are a top five "secrets" to making money investing, self-awareness must be among them. It is something important to which we need to pay attention. As we make trading decisions we often apply principles that work well in other areas of life. Sometimes we apply sports lessons like "It isn't over until the fat lady sings" (of course, the fat lady is likely to sing before the game). Hang in there, keep fighting, never give up are all things we have learned in other areas of life and that many try to apply, consciously or unconsciously, to our trading. The problem is that while these concepts might work well at work or in an athletic contest or in a battle, they may be devastating when applied to investments.

We need to be aware of our commitment to principles like those when we are investing. "I'll never give up, I'll keep fighting," translates into staying in a position even as it incurs greater and greater losses. That doesn't work very often. If an investment drops 50 percent in value, it must grow 100 percent just to break even. The "it isn't over until the fat lady sings" approach can result in violation of a very important principle—cut your losses. The difference between other things in life and the market is that we may be able to exercise some control by hanging in there at work, but unless we are a real power in finance or government, what we do has absolutely no effect on the market. It doesn't care. We have no influence so instead of hanging in there when an investment starts south, how about getting out of Dodge to make another play another day? We need to be aware of how much influence the "never give up" philosophy is a part of us and then learn to avoid investment mistakes because we may be trying to control something over which we have no control.

Another approach I have seen in many would-be traders and investors is that of the gambler. These folks seem to look at investing in the same way they might look at buying a lottery ticket. They look for the big win. At times, they may go "all in" on a position hoping it will bring them the big reward. They are classic examples of the get-rich-quick mentality. Once again, it is important to be aware of any inclination to be a gambler. Unless you are the house, the likelihood is that you will lose over time. In investing, the more successful participants work to make themselves the house. Rarely, if ever, do they "bet it all on black." Instead, they are aware of risk and manage money so that the risk overall and in any specific position is contained. Rather than trying to get rich quick, they work to get rich steady. They limit the size of any single position and they create streams of income as we have discussed throughout this book. If you want to gamble, my advice is to go to a casino with a limited amount of risk money, don't be a gambler with your investments. Awareness of a penchant to gamble can help a trader avoid the gamble and work with limited or hedged risk investments.

Risk awareness is critically important. Are you extremely conservative or do you consider yourself to be a daredevil? How will that influence your investing behavior? If you are afraid to take any risk then you probably should never try to cross a street or walk down a set of steps to go to work. Risk, literally, is everywhere. Few thought that the whole financial system of the United States could have reached the brink of disaster until it did. Who would have thought Lehman Brothers or Washington Mutual could fail almost overnight? Though there is always risk, throughout this book, we have looked at various ways in which we can attempt to limit it. Whatever our station in life, when we consider investments, we need to understand our individual reaction to risk and then measure that against the actual risk in entering any particular class of investment. The risk we take on will definitely have a bearing upon our well-being and ability to sleep at night. As we have seen, investments that produce income encompass a wide range of potential risk. We need to select those whose risk is in line with our personal tolerance. Our emotions here are a key to the level of risk we might be willing to take on. If we have that gnawing fear in the pit of our stomach, we are probably in an investment that is unsuitable for us. If we can be relaxed and comfortable with our positions, we probably are where we belong.

TURN THE KEY, START THE MACHINE: IT'S THE BEGINNING FOR YOU

We've reached a point where you have been exposed to a variety of ways you can add to your income. We've seen the relative risks of numerous approaches to improving your financial life. The future is about you and where you want to take it. Reading this book may have been an intellectual exercise or it may be the beginning of your work to construct a money machine in your own life.

I think it was Henry Ford who once said, "If you think you can or you think you can't, you are right." The fact is you can create added income for yourself. It won't make you instantly wealthy, but it can definitely add to the quality of your life. It isn't necessarily easy and it does require at least a little of your time. Only you can decide whether to take the next step. All I can say is be careful about depending on the government or a possible company pension to assure your financial future. What was once here may be gone. Witness Lehman Brothers, Enron, and a host of others whose employees expected decent retirement pensions. If you rely on yourself, you can improve your current situation and increase the likelihood of a more comfortable retirement. It is up to you.

Good luck and great success!

Options
Trading

The following material has been taken from Chapter 4 of my book, *Trade Your Way to Wealth* (John Wiley & Sons, 2008) in order to familiarize the reader with the basics of option trading. I have made some editorial changes from the material set out in the earlier book to fit the context here, but, for the most part, the language and certainly the concepts remain the same.

Options are contracts that give the buyer certain rights and place certain obligations on the seller. When we enter an option contract, we almost never know with whom we have contracted. We do not need to be concerned with who is on the other side of the option contract since the contract is guaranteed by the Option Clearing Corporation. All we need to know is that if we are the buyer of an option, we have certain rights. If we are the seller of an option, we have undertaken certain obligations. We do not have to worry about the enforcement of our rights since they are guaranteed by an independent organization. Table A.1 identifies the rights and obligations of buyers and sellers of calls and puts.

Generally, an options contract controls 100 shares of stock. Occasionally, an option contract controls a different number than 100 shares. Such a situation might arise, for example, when a stock has split 3:2. For that reason, you should always check before buying or selling an option contract

Reprinted with permission of John Wiley & Sons, Inc. *Trade Your Way to Wealth: Earn Big Profits with No-Risk, Low-Risk, and Measured-Risk Strategies* by Bill Kraft (John Wiley & Sons, 2008).

TABLE A.1 Option Trader Rights and Obligations

Action	Rights	Obligations
Buying Calls	Right to buy stock at the strike price anytime before expiration	
Selling Calls		Must sell stock at strike price before expiration if assigned (called) before options expire
Buying Puts	The right to force someone to buy stock at the strike price before expiration	
Selling Puts		Must buy stock at the strike price if assigned (put) before expiration

to make certain that you know how many shares actually will be controlled by the contract.

An option is defined by four separate criteria: (1) the identity of the underlying stock; (2) the strike price; (3) the expiration date; (4) whether the option is a put or call. Many, though not all, stocks have options. The stocks that do have options are generally those that trade more heavily. Naturally, the trader should always check to see whether the stock he is trading has or doesn't have options.

The strike price (sometimes called striking price) is the price at which the option can be exercised. For stocks priced below $30 or $35, the strike prices are generally $2.50 apart. For example, there may be strikes available at $22.50, $25, $27.50. Stocks that trade above $35 in price generally have strikes that are $5 apart such as $25, $30, $35. Higher priced stocks usually have their strikes $10 apart. Those guidelines are not set in stone so you will always want to check the option chain to see what strikes are available for the stock and options that interest you.

I should also note that some stocks such as the NASDAQ 100 Index Tracking Stock (QQQQ) and the Diamonds (DIA) have strikes that are only $1 apart. Strike prices are often referred to as "at the money," "in the money," and "out of the money." Oftentimes, these terms are confusing to traders, especially those who are unfamiliar with options. If a stock is trading at $50, both the $50 call and the $50 put are at the money. The at-the-money option is the strike nearest the price at which the stock is currently trading.

An option is considered to be "in the money" if it has intrinsic value. Intrinsic value is the built-in value or the part of the strike price of the option that is in the money. Probably the easiest way to see that is to look at a call option. Assume a stock is trading at $52 a share and we own the $50 call option. Since ownership of the call option gives us the right, but not the obligation, to buy the stock at any time up to expiration for $50 and the stock is already at $52, our call option would be $2 in the money. In other words, we could exercise our $50 call, buy the stock for $50, and immediately sell the stock on the open market for $52. Thus, it would have $2 built-in or intrinsic value.

A put option, on the other hand, provides the buyer with the right, but not the obligation, to force someone else to buy the stock at the strike price. If we owned a put option at a strike price of $50 we could force someone to buy our stock at $50 a share even if it were selling for less on the open market. If we owned a put option with a $50 strike price and the stock were only trading for $48 a share, our put option would be $2 in the money; in other words, it would have $2 of built-in or intrinsic value.

Out-of-the-money options on the other hand have no intrinsic value. Going back to the example of a call, suppose we own the $50 call option and the stock is selling on the open market for only $46 a share. We would have no reason to exercise our call option and buy the stock for $50 a share when we could buy it for $46 a share on the market. In that case, our $50 call would have no built-in or intrinsic value; it would only have time value. The same would be true if we owned a $50 put and the stock was trading at $51. We could sell our stock for $51 on the market in that instance so we would have no reason to "put" it (assign it) to someone for only $50. It would have no intrinsic value.

The following is a summary of at, in, and out of the money *calls*:

At the money = strike price closest to the current stock price

In the money = strike price of the call is lower than the current stock price (for example, a $45 call when the stock is trading at $48)

Out of the money = strike price of the call is higher than the current stock price (for example, a $50 call when the current stock price is $53)

The following summarizes at, in, and out of the money *puts*:

At the money = strike price closest to the current stock price

In the money = strike price of the put is higher than the current stock price (for example, a $50 put when the stock is trading at $47)

Out of the money = strike price of the put is lower than the current stock price (for example, a $50 put when the stock is trading at $52)

Option prices consist of two elements: intrinsic value and time value. Since the buyer is buying a right that will exist until expiration (unless he sells it first), he is in a position of control for that period of time and that right to control, over time, has value in and of itself. That portion of the option price is known as the time value. Suppose we bought a $50 call option for $2.50 with expiration three months away and suppose the stock was trading at exactly $50 when we bought the option. Would there be any intrinsic value at the time of the purchase? No, there would not be any intrinsic value since we could buy the same stock on the open market for $50 or we could exercise our call option and buy the stock for $50. Under that circumstance, the $2.50 premium we paid would all be time value. Now, let us assume that the stock rose in price over the next week or so to $54 a share and we still own the $50 call. Can you see that our call option now would have $4 in intrinsic value plus time value? It would have gone from an at-the-money option to an in-the-money option. Now our option might be worth say $6 ($4 intrinsic + $2 time). Of course, as time passes, the time value of an option usually diminishes. Since there is less time left until expiration, the time portion of the option price would have less value. Finally consider a strike price that is out of the money. Going back to the same example, we bought a $50 call option at the money when the stock was trading at $50. Some time passes and the price of the stock drops to $47.60. There would no longer be any intrinsic value. The premium for the option would drop since some time has passed and it has gained no intrinsic value. If we held on, the premium would eventually drop to zero as the option neared expiration. If we did not sell our option some time before expiration and it gained no intrinsic value, it would expire worthless.

Tables A.2 and A.3 give examples of the relationship between time value and intrinsic value.

If the preceding material is new to you, it may seem complex. If you get confused, just return to the tables and you will quickly become familiar with these concepts. Remember, this is a new language for you and you might need a little repetition for it to sink in completely. Believe me; the study you are performing now will definitely be worth it. Right now,

TABLE A.2   Calls with Stock Price at $25

In, At, or Out of the Money	Strike Price of Call	Total Premium	Intrinsic Portion	Time Value Portion
At the money	$25	$1.25	0	$1.25
In the money	$20	$5.75	$5	$0.75
Out of the money	$30	$0.50	0	$0.50

TABLE A.3 Puts with Stock Price at $25

In, At, or Out of the Money	Strike Price of Put	Total Premium	Intrinsic Portion	Time Value Portion
At the money	$25	$1.00	0	$1.00
In the money	$30	$5.40	$5	$0.40
Out of the money	$20	$0.25	0	$0.25

just remember that the premium you pay for an at-the-money or an out-of-the-money option is for time value only. The premium for an in-the-money option consists of both intrinsic value and time value. Also remember that you pay the highest premium for the time value portion of an option when you buy at-the-money options.

For all intents and purposes, the expiration of American-style options occurs at the *close* of market on the third Friday of the month. Technically, expiration actually occurs at noon on the Saturday following the third Friday of the month. However, for the retail trader, the close of business on the third Friday is the effective expiration. Most equity (stock) options have American-style expirations and can be exercised *at any time* before expiration. European-style options, on the other hand, cannot be exercised until expiration. While most stocks have American-style expirations, many indexes have European-style expirations. In some cases an index option may be settled on a cash basis calculated on the *opening* price on the third Friday of the month. While these European-style options may not be exercised until expiration, they may be traded up until expiration.

Utilities and Master Limited Partnerships

What follows is a list of optionable stocks and their dividend yield at the time I compiled the list in the summer of 2008. Check each stock and dividend before you take any action and do not rely on this information since the dividends may have been discontinued or changed up or down. Also check to determine whether they are still optionable at the time you are reviewing individual companies.

The lists include examples of equities that pay a dividend and are optionable in various sectors as of the time this Appendix was compiled and are not intended to be all-inclusive. They may help form some starting point for an individual investor's study and examination.

Electric Utilities

Allegheny Energy (AYE)	1.11%
American Electric Power (AEP)	3.8%
Black Hills Corp. (BKH)	3.94%
Cleco Corp. (CNL)	3.62%
Constellation Energy (CEG)	2.2%
Dominion Resources (D)	3.42%
DTE Energy (DTE)	4.8%
Duke Energy (DUK)	4.7%
Edison International (EIX)	2.3%
Entergy Corp. (ETR)	.5%
Firstenergy Corp. (FE)	2.8%
FPL Group (FPL)	2.7%
Great Plains Energy (GXP)	6.3%
Hawaiian Electric (HE)	4.65%
Idacorp Inc. Holding Co. (IDA)	3.85%
ITC Holdings Corp. (ITC)	2.1%
Nstar (NST)	4.2%
Oge Energy	4.2%
Ormat Technologies (ORA)	0.4%
Otter Tail Corp. (OTTR)	3.2%
Pepco Holdings (POM)	4.1%
Pinnacle West (PNW)	6.1%
PP&L Resources (PPL)	2.7%
Portland General Electric (POR)	4.1%
Progress Energy (PGN)	5.8%
Puget Sound Energy (PSD)	3.6%
Southern Company (SO)	4.5%
Teco Energy (TE)	4.1%
Unisource Energy (UNS)	2.9%
Xcel Energy (XEL)	4.3%

Gas Utilities

Agl Resources Inc. (ATG)	4.7%
Atmos Energy Corp. (ATO)	4.6%
Energen Corp. (EGN)	0.6%
Equitable Resources (EQT)	1.17%
National Fuel Gas Co. (NFG)	2%
Nicor Inc. (GAS)	4.7%
Northwest Natural Gas (NWN)	3.3%
Oneok Inc. (OKE)	3%
Sempra Energy (SRE)	2.1%
Southern Union Co. (SUG)	2.25%
Southwest Gas Corp. (SWX)	2.9%

Master Limited Partnerships

Alliance Resource Partners (ARLP)	5%
Amerigas Partners LP (APU)	7.4%
Buckeye Partners (BPL)	6.8%
Enbridge Energy Partners (EEP)	7.4%
Energy Transfer Partners (ETP)	6.9%
Ferrellgas Partners (FGP)	9%
Kinder Morgan Energy Partners (KMP)	6.3%
Magellan Midstreams Partners (MMP)	6.6%
Natural Resources Partners (NRP)	6.5%
Oneok Partners (OKS)	6.5%
Plains All American Pipeline (PAA)	7.3%
Suburban Propane Partners (SPH)	7.4%
Sunoco Logistics Partners (SXL)	6.8%

Real Estate Investment Trusts (REITs) with Options

T he following list of optionable REITs is neither exhaustive nor is it meant to recommend any specific REIT, but rather is intended only to provide examples of those investments in various segments of the real estate market:

Healthcare Facilities

HCP, Inc. (HCP)

Health Care Reit, Inc. (HCN)

Medical Properties Trust, Inc. (MPW)

Nationwide Health Prop. (NHP)

Ventas (VTR)

Hotel/Motel

Ashford Hospitality Trust, Inc. (AHT)

Diamondrock Hospitality Co. (DRH)

Felcor Lodging Trust, Inc. (FCH)

Host Hotels & Resorts, Inc. (HST)

Strategic Hotel & Resorts, Inc. (BEE)

Sunstone Hotel Investors, Inc. (SHO)

Industrial/Diversified

Alexandria Real Est. Eqts. (ARE)

Anthracite Capital, Inc. (AHR)

BioMed Realty Trust, Inc. (BMR)

Brandywine Realty Trust (BDN)

Cousins Properties, Inc. (CUZ)

Dct Industrial Trust, Inc. (DCT)

Digital Realty Trust, Inc. (DLR)

Douglas Emmett, Inc. (DEI)

Duke Realty Corp. (DRE)

Eastgroup Properties, Inc. (EGP)

Extra Space Storage (EXR)

National Retail Properties, Inc. (NNN)

Newcastle Investment (NCT)

Plum Creek Timber Reit (PCL)

Prologis (PLD)

Public Storage (PSA)

Rayonier (RYN)

Office

Boston Properties (BXP)

Liberty Property Trust (LRY)

Maguire Properties, Inc. (MPG)

Residential

American Campus Communities (ACC)

Apartment Invest. & Mgmt. (AIV)

Avalon Bay Communities (AVB)

BRE Properties, Inc. (BRE)

Education Realty Trust (EDR)

Equity Lifestyle Properties (ELS)

Equity Residential (EQR)

Essex Property Trust (ESS)

Home Properties, Inc. (HME)

Mid-America Apartment Communities, Inc. (MAA)

Senior Housing Properties Trust (SNH)

Udr, Inc. (UDR)

Retail

CBL & Assoc. Properties (CBL)

Developers Diversified (DDR)

Entertainment Prop. Trust (EPR)

Equity One, Inc. (EQY)

General Growth Props. (GGP)

Highwoods Properties, Inc. (HIW)

Hospitality Property Trust (HPT)

Hrpt. Properties Trust (HRP)

Inland Real Estate Corp. (IRC)

Kimco Realty Corp. (KIM)

Macerich Co. (MAC)

Northstar Realty Finance Corp. (NRF)

Pennsylvania Real Estate Investment Trust (PEI)

Post Properties, Inc. (PPS)

Realty Income Corp. (O)

Regency Centers Corp. (REG)

Resource Capital (RSO)

Simon Property Group (SPG)

SL Green Realty (SLG)

Taubman Centers, Inc. (TCO)

Vornado Realty Trust (VNO)

Washington Real Estate Investment Trust (WRE)

Weingarten Realty, Inc. (WRI)

Suggested Reading

W hat I have written in this book is the product of a great deal of reading and study as well as from hands-on experience. Much has been written about trading and investing and little is really new. I believe it is important for me to recognize some of the books and authors that have contributed to my own knowledge and enabled me to put together this book that attempts to show the reader how he can create additional income for himself in a variety of ways. For those people who may want to study more deeply, the list that follows includes a number of works that were helpful to me. I have also included my first book that may be valuable to you as well.

Block, Ralph L. *The Essential REIT*. San Francisco: Brunston Press, 1997.

Brandes, Michael V. *Naked Guide to Bonds*. New York: John Wiley & Sons, 2003.

Elder, Alexander. *Trading for a Living*. New York: John Wiley & Sons, 1993.

Hagstrom, Robert. *The Essential Buffett*. New York: John Wiley & Sons, 2001.

Kirkpatrick, Charles D. and Julie R. Dahlquist. *Technical Analysis: The Complete Resource for Technical Market Technicians*. New Jersey: FT Press, 2007.

Kiyosaki, Robert and Sharon Lechter. *Rich Dad, Poor Dad*. New York: Warner Books, 2000.

Kraft, Bill. *Trade Your Way to Wealth.* Hoboken: John Wiley & Sons, 2008.

Lefevre, Edwin. *Reminiscences of a Stock Operator.* New York: George H. Doran Company, 1923.

Lehman, Richard and Lawrence G. McMillan. *New Insights on Covered Call Writing.* Princeton: Bloomberg Press, 2003.

McMillan, Lawrence G. *Options as a Strategic Investment,* 4th edition. New York: New York Institute of Finance, 2002.

Nelson, Miles and Darlene Nelson. *Stock Split Secrets.* Seattle: Lighthouse, 2000.

Options Clearing Corporation. *Characteristics and Risks of Standardized Options* (pamphlet). Chicago: Author, 1987.

Sutton, Doug. *Beginning Investors Bible.* Seattle: Lighthouse, 2001.

Taleb, Nassim. *The Black Swan.* New York: Random House, 2007.

Thau, Annette. *The Bond Book,* 2nd edition. New York: McGraw-Hill, 2001.

Zweig, Jason. *Your Money & Your Brain.* New York: Simon & Schuster, 2007.

Index

J

Jobs, 6
Junk bonds, 130

K

Kiyosaki, Robert, 9

L

Laddering, 131–132
LEAPS. *See* Long Term Equity
    Anticipation Securities
Lechter, Sharon, 9
Lehman Brothers, 14
Lifestyle, xii
Long Term Equity Anticipation
    Securities (LEAPS), 59–67
    calendar spreads, 61–62
    calls to buy, 62
    calls to sell, 62–63
        examples, 63–64
    comparison between stock
        ownership and, 60–61
    if stock price falls, 64–65
    if stock price goes up, 64
    income appreciation, 66–67
    on splitting stocks, 65–66
Losses, 152–153

M

MarketFn.com, 153
Master Limited Partnerships
    (MLPs), 19, 23, 41–42,
    71–72, 149, 169
    benefits, 41–42
    cash distributions, 71
    liquidity, 72
    qualities, 41

risks, 41–42
tax advantages, 71–72
Maturity, 113
Medicare, 7
Merrill Lynch, 112
Microsoft (MSFT), 33
Middle-class, examples, 21–23,
    53–59
MLPs. *See* Master Limited
    Partnerships
Moody's, 116
MSFT. *See* Microsoft
Municipal bonds, 8, 19, 23, 126–128

N

Naked calls, selling, 94–102,
    102–105
    adjustments and exits, 97–100
    benefits, 94–95, 103–104
    combined with naked calls,
        105–110
    combined with naked puts,
        105–110
    requirements, 100–101, 104–105
    risks, 95–96, 102–103
    rules, 96–97, 104
    suitability, 101–102, 105
Naked puts. *See* Naked calls,
    selling
Naked straddle, 106–110
    adjusting, 107–108, 108–109
    naked strangles and, 108
    suitability, 109–110
Naked strangles
    naked straddles and, 108
    suitability, 109–110
NASDAQ, 162–163

O

1035 exchange, 142
Open-end funds, 75–76